I0487274

INVESTING IN BRAZIL!

INSTRUCTIONS

WHAT TO DO AND WHAT ...

NOT TO DO!!!

New Edition 2010
© Copyright Brazil Real Property 2008

All rights reserved

ISBN 978-1-4457-2687-8
90000

Introduction

In this practical and fast book have been collected the results of ten years of experience in terms of investments matured in Brazil, analyzing deeply every situation.

INVESTING IN BRAZIL
WHAT TO DO AND WHAT…NOT TO DO!
INSTRUCTIONS

It will let you get started already having a considerable experience of real estate investments so that you won't be victim of the myriad of "tricks" that you will inevitably run into, being aware of the rough truth.
Don't let your Paradise turn into your Hell…

You can choose!

CONTENTS

ABOUT BRAZIL

Brazil is a fascinating country with about 190 million inhabitants. It's the fifth largest country in the world and it's surrounded by all the South America's countries with the exception of Ecuador and Chile.

Brazilians are the essence of the country, in Brazil besides the wide range of ethnic groups belonging to different economic levels; the people have something in common: energy and passion.

Brazil has an excellent economic trend; nowadays it's the tenth major CDP (consumer of national products) in the world and one of the four greater developing economies (the other ones are China, India and Russia).

"By 2050 it will be the fifth biggest economy in the world".
Source. Goldman Sachs.

Brazil has something for everybody, whether you are looking for a good place to invest in real estate, a safe and healthy place to retire or spend 6 months in the sun or holiday.

Brazil has almost everything you could imagine, sailing, surfing, fishing, diving, kite surfing. rafting or any other activity sport you could imagine. Alternatively if you fancy whale or dolphin watching, beautiful scenery and wildlife; Brazil will amaze you. For those whose passion is football, Formula One or volleyball, golf or almost any other sport you can imagine, Brazil has it all.

Brazil makes good sense for real estate because you have excellent legal rights and few restrictions to investing in real estate and Brazil will become one of the leading economies in the world in the next 20 years. Of course selecting the right location and property is always important.

The combination of macroeconomic and institutional stability, sustained growth, strong social inclusion and income distribution policies have launched a new Brazil onto the international scene. These changes, in conjunction with one of the most modern and solid financial systems, and together with a strict balancing of the federal budget and a strong domestic market has made Brazil more resistant than most countries to the effects of the present international financial crisis.

Taming inflation, balancing the federal budget and a vigorous program of social inclusion are factors that have driven a new cycle of expansion, supported by an important investment plan in infrastructure and public education.

The Brazilian economy rests on strong fundamentals: inflation at 5% annually, sustainable economic growth of around 4% annually and fiscal stability, with a primary federal budget surplus of 4.1% of GDP in 2008.

Brazil is a federal republic, with a presidential system of government.

It has a consolidated democratic system, with free elections every two years, with checks and balances between the executive, legislative and judicial branches. It is a country that lives in peace and cooperates with its neighbors. Brazil is signatory to the major international treaties, and open to foreign investment.

Industrial parks

Continental in size, with its 8.5 million square kilometers (fifthlargest country in the world), Brazil has high tech centers throughout the country, from the modern petrochemical complex in Rio Grande do Sul, the country's southernmost state, moving north past the high tech cluster of São Paulo, to Bahia, in the Northeast, where Ford operates the most modern automobile factory in the world.

And in the cerrado (savannah) region, on the Midwest plains, a high technology and productivity complex is operating at full steam. Investment in research and development, under the leadership of the Brazilian Agricultural Research Corporation (Embrapa), has made agribusiness in Brazil one of the most modern and productive in the world. The capacity to innovate also has enabled Brazil to lead the way in deep sea petroleum exploration. Today Petrobras, state-owned energy company, in addition to exploring deposits in other parts of the world, embarks on a new challenge: that of doubling reserves, by exploring underwater deposits beneath the deep sea layer, which will place the country among the top five producers in the world.

Stability

The current scenario is one of stability and economic predictabi-lity, which has allowed Brazil to garner investment-grade status from the major credit rating agencies. The Brazilian institutional environment ensures security for investors, who also benefit from a modern and efficient financial system, with a special role played by the Brazilian Development Bank (BNDES) of the Federal Government, which financed economic development of about US$ 40 billion in 2008, topping the amount disbursed by the World Bank (US$ 13.4 billion) and the Inter-American Development Bank (US$ 12.2 billion) together. As Brazil is a full member of World Trade Organization, BNDES is ready to finance development projects of any foreign owned company in Brazil.

The Brazilian industrial park is diversified: including industrial goods companies (such as steel factories and petroleum refineries) and consumer goods (automobiles, textiles, etc.).

Factories that produce anything from rubber flip-flops to airplanes.

It is self-sufficient in petroleum and is one of the most important world producers of ethanol from sugarcane. The already well developed Brazilian service sector is responsible for 56.3% of Gross Domestic Product as is normally found in more developed economies.

One of the main reasons for the success of Brazil was its ability to balance sustainable economic growth with social inclusion. In recent years, millions of Brazilian men and women have entered the domestic consumer market and strengthened their citizenship in the process. The percentage of Brazilians who live in extreme poverty fell from 8.8% of the population in 1990, to 4.2%, in 2005. In 2007, for the first time, the United Nations (UN) included Brazil in the group of countries with the highest degree of human development.

Market expansion

The consumer market has expanded, attracting new entrepreneurs and expanding business. Roughly 20 million Brazilians have migrated from income brackets D and E to C, from 2002 to 2007. Consumers from the C income bracket, the middle class, are today estimated to number 97 million, or around 52% of the country's population. These advances are the result of policies to recoup salary purchasing power, greater access to credit and priority investments in education, health, and poverty fighting initiatives in the city and in rural areas, with special emphasis on the Bolsa Família income transfer program.

In addition to a domestic market undergoing expansion, the country is a robust export platform. Its share of world trade has risen from 0.9% in 2000 to 1.2% in 2007, with exports rising from US$ 55.1 billion to US$ 160.6 billion over the same period. Brazilian companies are also gaining ground abroad, due to their presence throughout the world

and position at the forefront of various sectors. They are truly world-class companies. Brazil's positive trade balance and the flow of productive investment have contributed to building foreign currency reserves, which reached US$ 206.8 billion at the end of 2008.

Brazil also ensures a secure and diversified supply of energy, which is one of its greatest competitive advantages. Renewable sources such as electricity generated by hydroelectric, wind power and biomass plants provide 44% of energy needs – a world record.

Abroad, Brazilian foreign policy has opened borders and established solid partnerships in various regions of the world, thereby diversifying exports. Brazil has strengthened Mercosur by promoting integration with its South American neighbors and improving relations with traditional partners, such as the United States and Europe. While at the same time, it has expanded trade with Africa, Asia and Arab countries.

The dramatic transformations that have occurred in Brazil over the last twenty years have made the country the preferred destination for Brazilian and international investors. In 2008, productive foreign investment rose to a record of US$ 45.1 billion, second only to China among developing countries.

The country consolidates its position in the global economy, by participating decisively in the primary international forums that are used to address commercial, environmental, technological and public safety issues.

MAPS

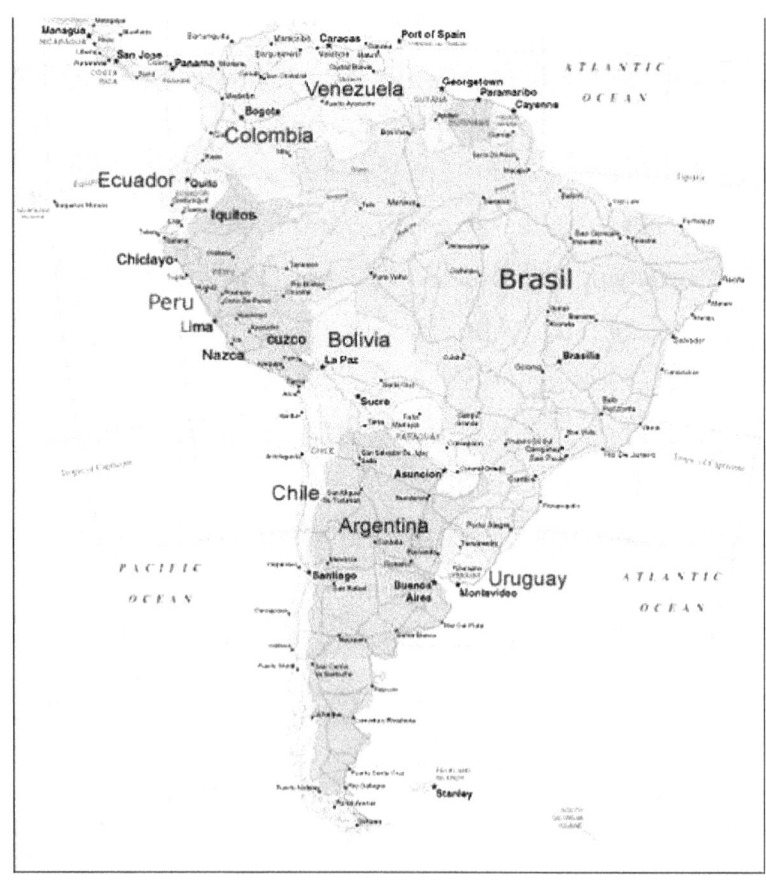

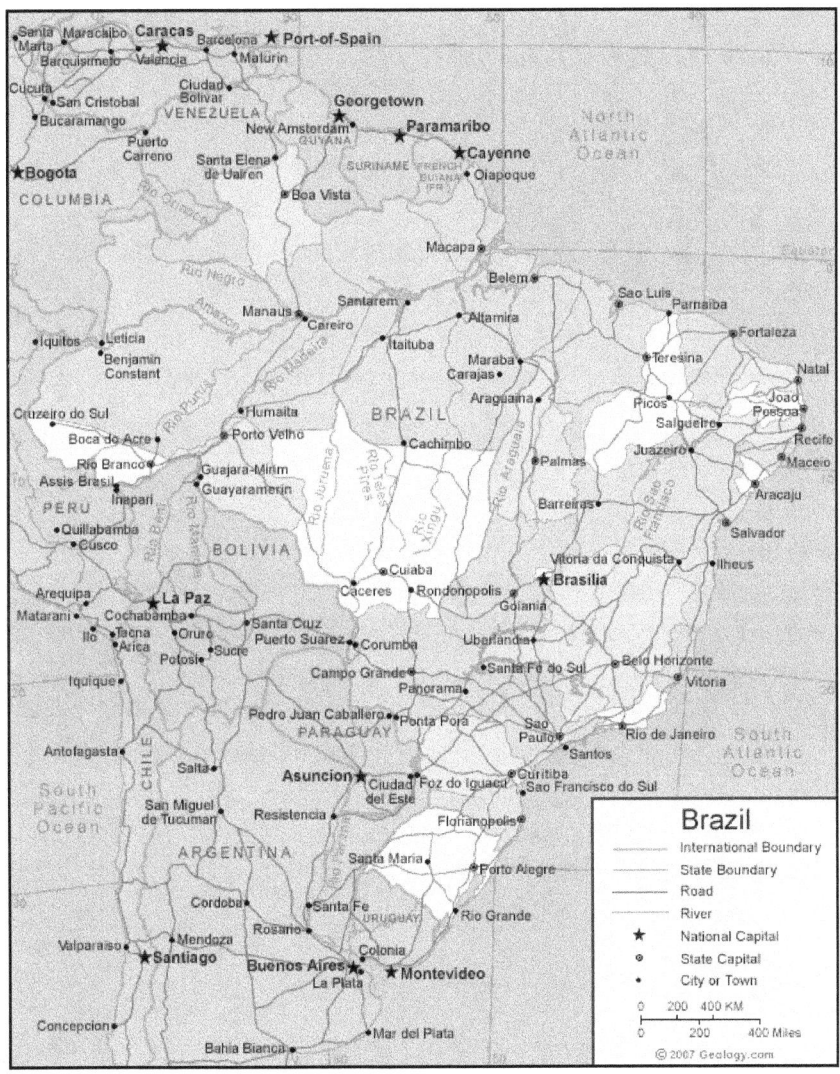

Roraima
Amapá
Amazonas
Pará
Ceará
Rio Grande do Norte
Maranhão
Acre
Rondônia
Tocantins
Piauí
Paraíba
Pernambuco
Alagoas
Sergipe
Mato Grosso
Bahia
Goiás
Distrito Federal
Mato Grosso do Sul
Minas Gerais
Espírito Santo
São Paulo
Rio de Janeiro
Paraná
Santa Catarina
Rio Grande do Sul

Regiões

Norte

Nordeste

Centro-Oeste

Sudeste

Sul

Mapa 1.16
Unidades Climáticas do Brasil

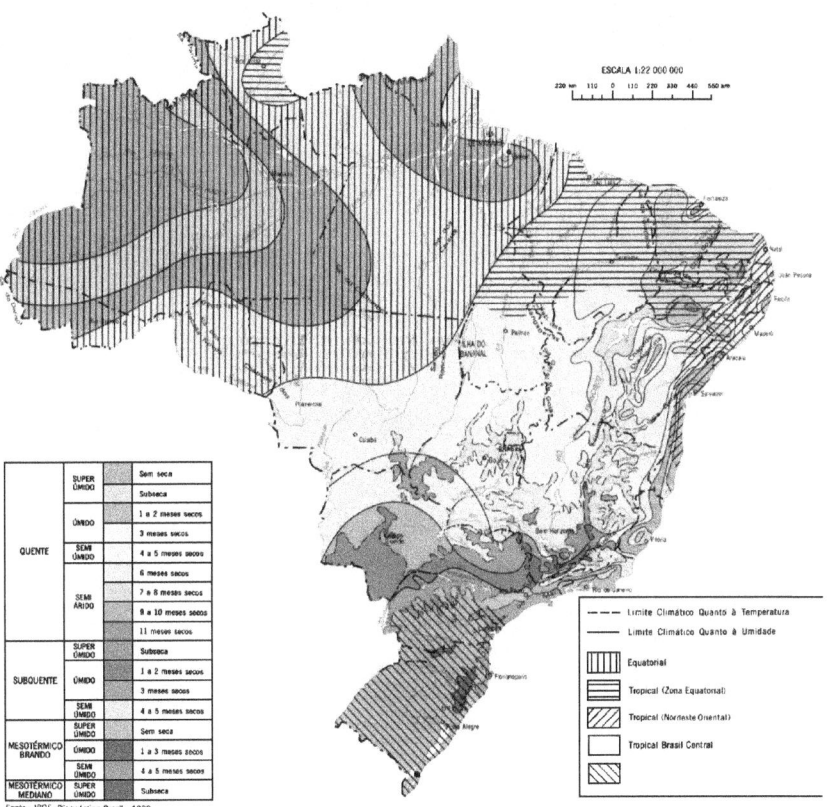

ESCALA 1:22 000 000

220 km 110 0 110 220 330 440 550 km

QUENTE	SUPER ÚMIDO		Sem seca
			Subseca
	ÚMIDO		1 a 2 meses secos
			3 meses secos
	SEMI ÚMIDO		4 a 5 meses secos
			6 meses secos
	SEMI ÁRIDO		7 a 8 meses secos
			9 a 10 meses secos
			11 meses secos
SUBQUENTE	SUPER ÚMIDO		Subseca
	ÚMIDO		1 a 2 meses secos
			3 meses secos
	SEMI ÚMIDO		4 a 5 meses secos
MESOTÉRMICO BRANDO	SUPER ÚMIDO		Sem seca
	ÚMIDO		1 a 3 meses secos
	SEMI ÚMIDO		4 a 5 meses secos
MESOTÉRMICO MEDIANO	SUPER ÚMIDO		Subseca

Fonte - IBGE, Diagnóstico Brasil - 1990

- - - Limite Climático Quanto à Temperatura

——— Limite Climático Quanto à Umidade

Equatorial

Tropical (Zona Equatorial)

Tropical (Nordeste Oriental)

Tropical Brasil Central

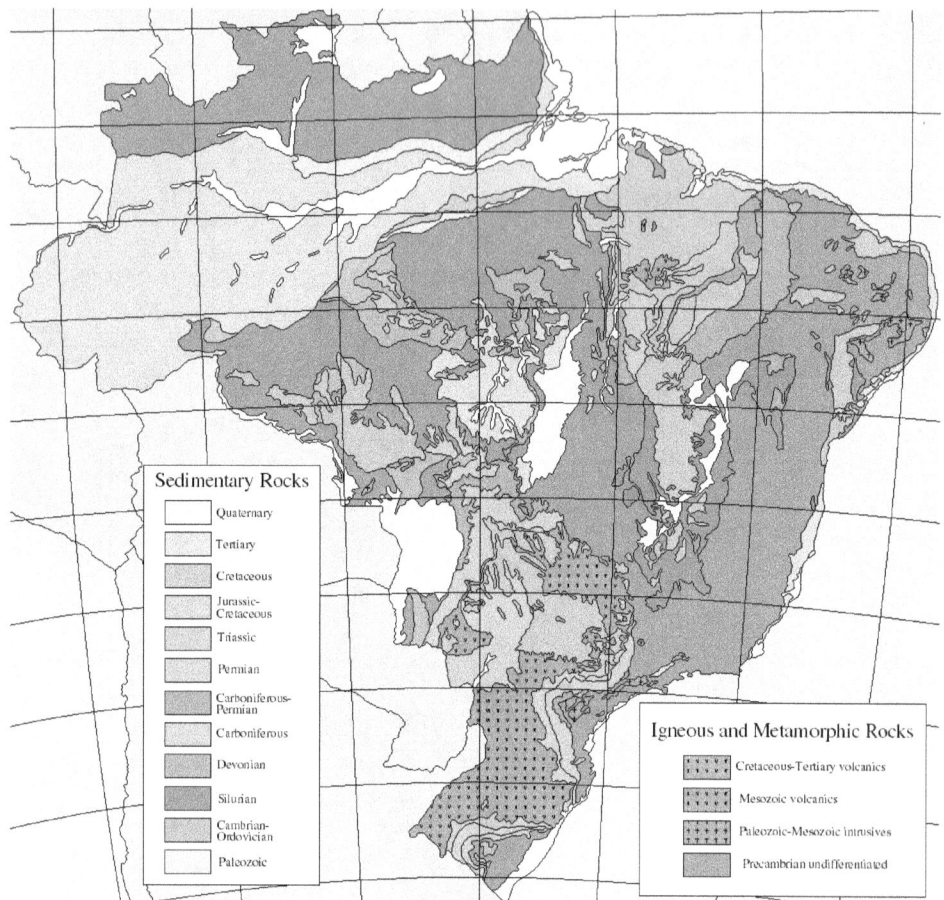

Sedimentary Rocks

- Quaternary
- Tertiary
- Cretaceous
- Jurassic-Cretaceous
- Triassic
- Permian
- Carboniferous-Permian
- Carboniferous
- Devonian
- Silurian
- Cambrian-Ordovician
- Paleozoic

Igneous and Metamorphic Rocks

- Cretaceous-Tertiary volcanics
- Mesozoic volcanics
- Paleozoic-Mesozoic intrusives
- Precambrian undifferentiated

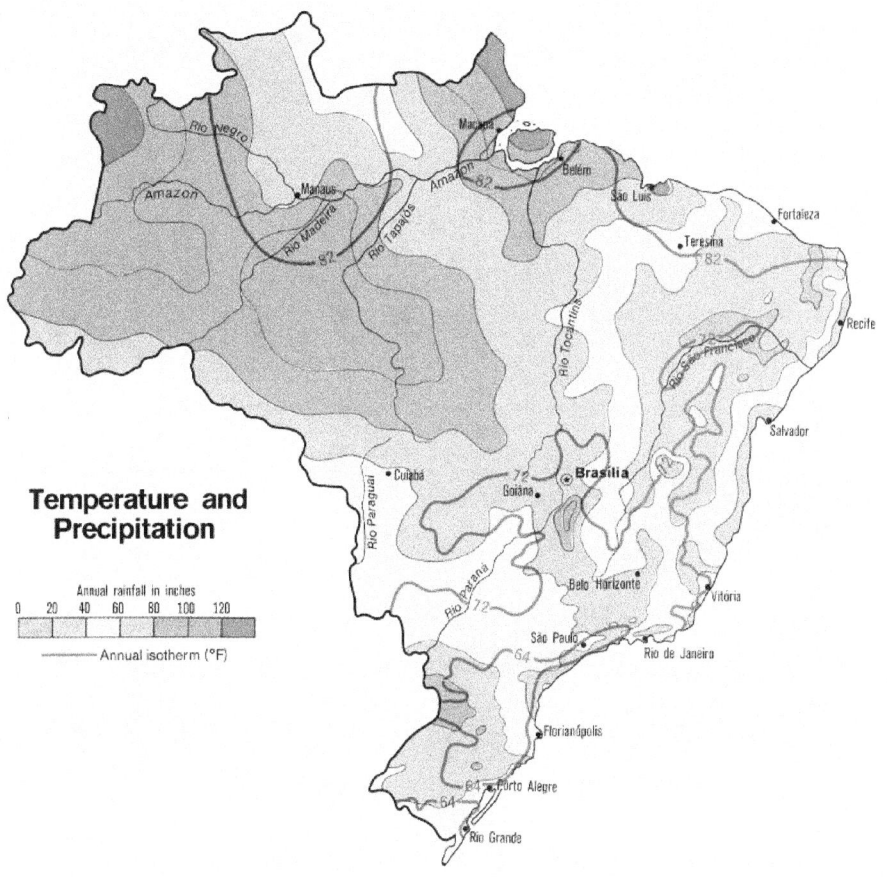

Temperature and Precipitation

Annual rainfall in inches

0   20   40   60   80   100   120

Annual isotherm (°F)

Cajueiro
Calcanhar
Touros
Rio do Fogo
Zumbi
Punaú
Pititinga
Coconho
Maracajaú
Caraúbas
Cabo de São Roque
Maxaranguape
Muriú
Jacumá
Pitangui

Praias Norte

Barra do Rio
Genipabú
Santa Rita
Redinha

Rio Potengi

NATAL

Praias
Centrais

Praia do Forte

Praia do Meio

Ponta do Morcego

Areia Preta

Barreira Roxa

Ponta Negra

Pium
Cotovelo
Pirangi do Norte

Praias Sul

Pirangi do Sul

Bonfim

Búzios

Tabatinga

Camurupim

Lagoas

Barreta

Tibau do Sul

Guaíra

Pipa

Cunhaú

Baía Formosa

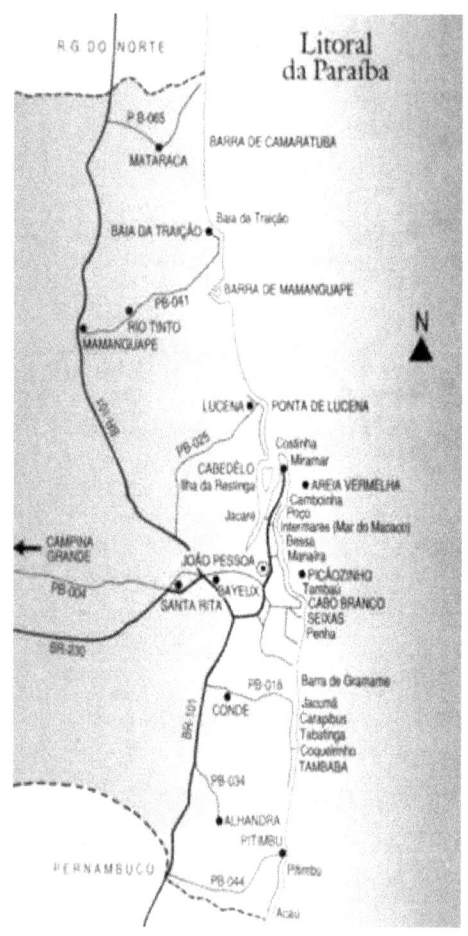

GOIANA
- Carne de Vaca
- Catuama
- Pontas de Pedra
- Pontal da Ilha
- Atapuz
- Do Fortinho
- Lance dos Cações
- Do Sossego
- Jaguaribe
- Pilar

ITAMARACÁ
- Quatro Cantos / Baixa Verde
- do Rio Âmbar / Forno da Cal
- Forte Orange
- Coroa do Avião
- Da Gavoa

IGARASSU
- Maria Farinha
- Conceição

PAULISTA
- Pau Amarelo
- Janga

OLINDA
- Casa Caiada
- Bairro Novo
- Do Farol
- Milagres
- Del Chifre

RECIFE
- Porto do Recife
- Do Pina
- Boa Viagem
- Piedade

JABOATÃO
- Candeias
- Ilha do Amor
- Du Paiva
- Itapuama

CABO
- Pedra do Naréu
- Enseada dos Corais
- Gaibu
- Calhetas
- Cabo de Stº Agostinho

IPOJUCA
- Paraíso
- Suape
- Muro Alto
- Camboa
- Porto de Galinhas
- Maracaipe
- Serrambi

SIRINHAÉM
- Cacimbas

RIO FORMOSO
- Toquinho
- Barra de Sirinhaém
- Da Gamela
- Guadalupe

TAMANDARÉ
- Dos Carneiros
- Tamandaré

BARREIROS
- Boca da Barra
- Do Porto

SÃO JOSÉ DA COROA GRANDE
- Várzea de Una
- Gravatá
- São José da Coroa Grande

Litoral de Pernambuco

DIVERSITY: CULTURAL AND NATURAL ASSETS

Brazil is a country of many origins, with the arrival of people from every part of the world, which fostered an environment of tolerance and cultural diversity.

Brazil fascinates with the miscegenation of its indigenous, European, Asian and African roots and the reflection of these various facets on its culture. The cuisine, music, folk art, architecture, artistic expression and popular festivities travel beyond the country's borders. Brazil has 17 cultural and natural assets protected as Unesco World Heritage Sites and one of the marvels of the contemporary world, the Christ the Redeemer statue. Brazil is a country of ethnic, cultural, religious and social tolerance.

Instead of hostility, a large number of ethnic groups find in Brazil an environment of respect and tolerance of differences, open to exchanging experiences. This creates a

social environment where Brazilians absorb pluralism and the respect for differences and exchange experiences. This peaceful coexistence leads to versatile and highly original cultural manifestations. Diversity is also present in its architectural jewels, from the colonial baroque period to the modernism of Brasília, the capital.

Immigration in Brazil was extremely important for the formation of national culture. Characteristics from the four corners of the world were incorporated over the five centuriessince the arrival of the Portuguese in 1500. In additionto the contributions by Indians, Africans and Portuguese,the substantial number of immigrants from Europe, theMiddle East and Asia has influenced the formation of the Brazilian people. Immigration from neighboring countries, such as Argentina, Uruguay, Chile and Bolivia, has also contributed to the diversification of customs, habits and beliefs, but with a common language.

Despite Brazil's vast territory, all of its regions speak the same language. Portuguese is the fifth most spoken language in the world and the third among Western languages, after English and Spanish.

The Brazilian Constitution guarantees the full exercise of cultural rights and states that the government must support, promote and value its manifestations, in addition to protecting the indigenous, African-Brazilian and other cultures that have contributed to the country's civilization.

The Brazilian indigenous population is 565,000 and increases at a rate higher than the national average. Various affirmative action programs promote equality and protection of rights of individuals and racial and ethnic groups affected by discrimination and other forms of intolerance, with an emphasis on the black population. The goal is to put into practice emancipatory government policies by 2010 for the communities of slave descendants located in 330 towns in 22 Brazilian states.

In addition to its rich and mixed culture, Brazil is a continent- sized country that offers 8,000 kilometers of sunny and beautiful beaches, along with numerous natural attractions for ecotourism and leisure. Brazil has the potential to attract tourists of all segments and styles. The country's good infrastructure, its cultural variety, the hospitality of its people and its natural beauty allow it to compete in various segments of the international tourism market.

But the greatest Brazilian asset is its people, formed by various cultures that live in harmony. There are close to 190,6 million inhabitants in the fifth most populous country in the world. Most of its population is still young, unlike many other economies.

ECONOMY IN THE FUTURE

The strongest promoter of the recent development of the country has been the 2003 administration. This long-lasting new government has created a favorable economy for foreign investments adopting both a fiscal and a modernization policy that lead to solid commercial growth.

WHY BRAZIL

- the friendly and hospitable people

- the beautiful country

- the lovely beaches

- the perfect weather and climate - no hurricanes, tsunamis, no earthquakes, and in the North East you have warm sunny

- weather all year round

- the exceptional value for money for shopping, eating out and low cost of living

- good investment opportunity

- the strong performance of the economy, with robust growth and a trade surplus

- the great nightlife

- the choice of food

- sports

- exceptional customer service (where else can you have a pharmacy deliver your medicines at 4am)

- the relaxed pace of life

- Brazil is an excellent choice for living and for spending holidays with a terrific quality of life.
- The climate is constant during the whole year with an average temperature of 27 degrees.

TOO EXPENSIVE FOR YOU? HERE ARE THE FACTS…

- You can buy a property by the sea cheaper than 50.000€/67.000$
- A dinner for two people in a good quality restaurant including wine is 10€/14$
- A bottle of Brazilian beer is 73cents€/99cents$

Many people that visit Brazil come back over and over again. There are many and various reasons for this:

- Because of the hospitality and the happiness of the Brazilian people
- The beauty of the country
- The breathtaking beaches
- The perfect climate, in the northeast it's warm all year long
- The favorable exchange rate for shopping and eating and also because of the low cost of life
- Fast growing economy
- Magnificent night life
- The good quality food
- Because of the great variety of sports

PROSPECTIVE

The Brazilian government looks at tourism as one of its greater resources and promotes it ardently. The minister of tourism settled down in 2003 and began to promote the potential of the country as a destination for domestic and international vacations. The number of tourists has increased from 3,7 millions of 2002 to 5,5 million in 2005.This is an awesome increase of 48% and a reason for investors to celebrate.

TOURISM

Brazil received over 5 million tourists in 2008, a similar figure to 2007 and its National Plan for Tourism aims to increase this figure to 9 million visitors a year in the near future, creating 1.2 million new jobs.

According to the World Travel and Tourism Council (WTTC), Brazil's tourism industry, the biggest in South America, rose to 13th position in terms of the economic activity it generates. Tourism in Brazil is expected to contribute US$82.8 billion to the economy in 2009. The WTTC also predicts the sector will expand at an average annual rate of 4.5% between 2010 and 2019.

Travel and tourism currently account for nearly 6% of employment in Brazil (around 5.5 million jobs), and that is forecast to rise substantially when Brazil hosts the World Cup in 2014.

Brazil is world renowned for its myriad of attractions including its 7,400km of tropical beaches, the wonders of the Amazon rainforest and the vibrancy of its people and culture. The north east region of Brazil, centred around the resort of Natal, is increasingly popular with tourists, particularly Brazil's wealthy population, and major investment (over US$1.8 billion) in new hotels, golf courses and resorts is underway in the area.

OBJECTIVES

With the governmental plan of economic expansion it has been invested more than $736 million in infrastructure, such as expansions of airports, restoration of important historical sites and different environmental preservation projects.

The main aims of the Brazilian Governmental expansion plan in tourism are:

- Attracting more than 9 million visitors per year
- Creating 1.200.000 new jobs
- Receiving 8 billion dollars in foreign investments
- Diversify tourism offering investors new projects such as rural and Eco-sport tourism.
- Increasing the average spend of each tourist
- Increasing domestic flights to 5 million per year
- In a recent survey 96% of tourists visiting Brazil have stated that will come back to the Samba country!

BRAZILIAN CITIES

Regardless of whether this is your first visit to Brazil, or your one hundredth, the fact is that Brazil offers so many different things for the tourist to do and see there is neither a best time nor a best place! So, to try and help you plan your Brazil holiday around some of Brazil's spectacular sights and wonders, here are the top things to do in brazil (in no particular order of preference):

AMAZONIA NATIONAL PARK

Covering an impressive 7 of Brazil's 27 states, "The Green Inferno" covers almost 40 per cent of Brazil's total landmass. Although parts of the Amazon cover countries bordering Brazil (notably Bolivia, Colombia, Guiana and Peru), it is to Brazil that most tourist come if they want to take in the splendors of this most magnificent natural wonder. Things to do in the Amazon include bird watching, trekking/hiking, climbing and taking boat journeys along the river. Without doubt, a tour to Brazil is incomplete without a trip to the Amazon.

IGUASSU FALLS OR IGUACU FALLS

Sometimes described as being one of the 7 natural Wonders of the World; in fact, Iguassu Falls are neither the widest waterfall in the world, nor are they the tallest. However, what it lacks in width and height it makes up for elsewhere. On the Parana River, the falls act as a natural border to the countries of Brazil, Argentina and Paraguay and compose of 275 cataracts in total. Best time of year to see the Iguacu Falls is between October and December and as this is such a magnificent sight, it is highly recommended that you make arrangements to stay at least one night here before moving on to your next destination!

RIO DE JANEIRO

The word exotic sums up Rio! But, Rio is also chaotic, sophisticated, open, friendly, busy and relaxed. It's literally is everything rolled up into one! Most people see Rio as sun, sea, and surf. Whilst Rio is all of these, it is also much more. As Brazil second most populous city (after Sao Paulo), Rio is also highly regarded as being the educational and cultural center of Brazil - with both some of Brazil's leading universities and some of the most delightful museums and art galleries.

If you're seeking a combination of beaches, sports, sun, exotic parks and gardens, spectacular mountain views, plus a bit of dancing and drinking, Rio is for you. Rio de Janeiro has a majestic beauty, nestled between a glorious bay with dazzling beaches and a sharply rising mountain range covered by tropical vegetation.

With the establishment of Brasilia in 1960, Rio ceased to be Brazil's capital, but this second largest city is still a major cultural capital with museums housing a wide range of art and information on Brazilian life and culture. The city is one of the most densely populated on earth, with 6 million inhabitants.

Rio Beach Rio loves the sun and its world famous beaches are free to all, with surfing is popular pastime. The legendary Copacabana beach is lively, with people often playing beach volleyball with the samba playing in the background. The sidewalks are filled with drink stands and peddlers hawking everything imaginable you might need.

Another beach, Ipanema, is known for its attraction to the young and fashionable, with numerous boutiques. Joggers and children of the wealthy hang out here.

Museu Historico National On the cultural side, Rio's museums and privately funded cultural centers are filled with masterpieces and wonderful history. The Museu Historico National boasts a collection of 30,000 items, including ivory toys once owned by the imperial family. At the Mosteiro de Sao Bento you can view a richly adorned interior with magnificent silver chandeliers and ceiling paintings dedicated to the Virgin. A Franciscan convent is paneled in gilded wood, with painted ceilings depicting the glorification of Saint Francis.

It would take a full day to seek out all the large churches, but tours cover many of them. A highlight is the baroque Igreja de Nossa Senhora da Gloria do Outeiro. Overlooking the city, it's known for its large dome, ornamental stonework, and vivid tile work.

One of the most thrilling sites is Corcovado, a mountain with a sheer granite face topped by the Cristo Redentor (Christ the Redeemer) statue rising more than 100 feet from a 20-foot pedestal. You can reach the top on an 1885 cogwheel train or on a winding road with great beach views.

Sugarloaf Mountain The second famous peak, Sugarloaf Mountain, is just as impressive, giving a different perspective of the city. Sugarloaf consists of a huge granite slab at the entrance of the Guanabara Bay. From the top at 1,295 feet, (photo 50-4), you can see the whole city, plus the beaches and the Atlantic Ocean. To ascend, you catch a two-stage cableway with a length of 4,265 feet. The sunsets as seen from the top are fabulous. (brazil-rio-sugarloaf-mountain2.jpg)

The city's festive life comes to a head during the annual Carnaval, which is enjoyed by the entire city for three solid day. Music, partying, balls, street parades, brilliantly costumed dancers--you name it.

Hints and Resources

And, of course, there's always Carnival and samba time in Rio! Carnival is the best time to visit the city, if you don't mind if it's even more crowded. Carnival takes place in February or March, depending on the date of Easter each year. It's best to arrive a bit early to enjoy all the sights. And, most important, book your hotel at least a year in advance.

Things to Avoid

Sunburn: The sun is powerful here and rays can burn your skin in a very short time. Use sunscreen liberally.

Theft

Be especially careful at the beaches and at night. Leave your passport, jewelry, and most cash at your hotel.

PANTANAL

Considered one of the world's great wildlife reserves, any tour to the Pantanal needs to be carefully planned as the area is not ideally suited to the tourist - with little infrastructure in place. However, don't let this stop you from making arrangements to visit the Pantanal as this is truly a splendid place. Fishermen will also be attracted to the Pantanal as it has some of the best fishing in South

America. But, it is for the birds that most visitors come to the Pantanal and bird watching here is truly amazing!

SALVADOR

Formerly Brazil's colonial capital city, the city of Salvador is located on the Bay of All Saints. Visitors to this wonderful city can revel in walking the narrow cobblestone streets that have changed little since the days when the city served as the slave center of Brazil.

Visitors to Salvador are also strongly encouraged to take a visit to the Igreja de Sao Francisco. The interior of this otherwise unremarkable church is covered in gold leaf. Not too far away from the church is the Farol de Barra, a 16th Century fortified lighthouse overlooking the second biggest bay in Brazil!

However, visitors to Brazil looking to see some of Brazil's colonial past are strongly advised to make the journey to Salvador, where they'll be enthralled with 17th century antiques on display at the Museu de Arte da Bahia and Museu de Arte Sacra.

The city of Salvador, the capital of colonial Brazil for almost two centuries, is today a city of 2 million people. The black African culture, originating with former slaves, is reflected strongly in the city's culture. In fact, 70 percent of the city's population is Afro-

Brazilian and ceremonies honor both African gods and Catholic holidays.

The city was built two distinct levels, with residences in the hills and office buildings below, and today it is still divided into upper and lower cities, with an elevator to take you from one to another.

Salvador's beaches have been an inspiration for writers and musicians. They provide chairs and umbrellas at kiosks selling a range of tempting food. Many beaches are lit up at night and boast bars and restaurants for the evening crowd.

Perhaps you'll want to spend time shopping at the grand Mercado Modelo or visiting numerous museums. Or, you could venture out to Forte de Santo Antonio at the tip of the peninsula, and wander through the lighthouse or the nautical museum, or maybe enjoy the nearby beach.

Hotel choices in Salvador are ample and range from elegant high-rises to family-run apartments. Public transportation to various parts of the city is available at the bottom of the small hill on which the hotel is located.

Hints

The best time to visit the city is between November and April and the month of July (when schools are out).

Things to Avoid

It's best not to wander around at night, particularly if you're alone. And, of course, watch your belongings carefully.

SAO PAULO

There is one word that sums up Sao Paulo - "BIG"! The city is not only the most populous in all Brazil, but as the commercial center of Brazil it also contains some of the biggest skyscrapers in the country. However, visitors to Sao Paulo should not be mistaken into believing that Sao Paulo is all work and no play, once the sun has set Sao Paulo likes to party at some of the trendiest pubs and clubs in all of Brazil - some argue that Sao Paulo's clubs are more in-tune with western and modern styles than Rio!

Sao Paulo, Brazil is one of the countries most splendid jewels. This gem is a radiant city, alive with culture and industry. 45 miles from the Atlantic coast, Sao Paulo (which stands from St. Paul in Portuguese) is an amalgam of the various cultures that shape the face of this modern, bustling Brazilian metropolis.

The city of Sao Paulo, despite being so populous today, remained for hundred of years a smaller colonial town, evident in the relics of the old city that can still be found all over Sao Paulo.

Today, 32 malls, hundreds of boutiques and scores of fine stores line the busy streets of this prosperous city. It is also proud to be the home of 2 of 15 of he world's finest zoos, as well as a great number of parks and a magnificent botanical garden.

Sao Paulo has the best of both worlds, with virtually everything you could want to find in a large city, as well as some things you wouldn't expect. One notable fact is the large immigrant population, giving this centuries old metropolis a cosmopolitan and diverse face. The over 1 million Japanese who live here give this city the notable distinction of being the largest Japanese city outside Japan. Liberdade is the name of the neighborhood where you can find this hub of Japanese culture - it is a center of the Asian community, enhanced by the quaint gardens and exotic shops.

To add to the cultural wealth of Sao Paulo, Brazil, the museums here have some of the best permanent exhibits of Latin American art and architecture anywhere in the South American continent. The contemporary profile of a half dozen buildings of The Latin American Memorial Complex is replete with Latin American art. This complex is easily accessed via the clean and modern subway system, one of the world's finest.

Marvel at the exquisite furnishings of Brazils imperial era at the Ipiranga Imperial Museum (Museu Paulista), another one of Sao Paulo's cultural highlights. With so many resources and modern conveniences, this city is a delight to live as well as to explore. The wide boulevards of Paulista Avenue, Sao Paulo's main street, is a great place to start exploring the city of foot, and is a busy center of commerce and tourism.

Sao Paulo is a fascinating juxtaposition of old and new - here you can find colonial era splendor set against modern comforts. Sao Paulo is a city that begs to be explored. Clean, bright, and exciting, this city will completely revolutionize your ideas of the country of Brazil.

BRASILIA

Brasilia was constructed by the country's leading architects, Oscar Niemeyer and Lucio Costa, in the 1950s to replace Rio as Brazil's capital city - which it did in 1960. That, however, doesn't mean the city's design has been well thought-out - it hasn't! To be fair, Brasilia was intended as the administrative capital of Brazil, a function it serves well to this day. However, the city's planners had not taken into consideration any private enterprise existing in Brasilia. Consequently all of the architects' good intentions went out of the window and the city is little more than a sprawling mess of modern building design. As such a new city, the city also lacks from having any real claim to heritage. All in all then, Brasilia is certainly worth a visit if you have the time, but if your time is restricted, go to all the other places first!

MANAUS

Located right in heart of the Amazonian Basin, Manaus is a popular destination for tourists looking for excursions into the exotic heartland of the Amazon. However, what was once considered to be one of the greatest wilderness outposts in the world is, as a result of years of over construction, no longer able to claim this title.

Nonetheless, Manus does offer two great attractions to its tourist visitors. The first is obviously the chance to travel further into the Amazon Basin, the second is the chance to see some of the world's largest sea-going ships come to port some one thousand miles inland, where they load and unload their wares (which are then taken, or brought from, further inside the Amazon!).

RECIFE

Located on the Gold Coast of Brazil (northeastern Brazil), Recife is a famous tourist destination for the package tourist. Recife is also well known for the number of canals and bridges that criss-cross this city. The city also has a number of good museums and churches. However, no visit to Recife is complete without a visit to the town's old prison - to make your visit there more interesting, it's now a shopping complex!

Recife is the capital of Pernambuco in Brazil and is considered a fairly major port city. Recife is the fifth largest city in Brazil but is less modern and cosmopolitan than some other major Brazilian cities. In Recife Brazil, the Beberibe River meets up with the Capibaribe River and flows swiftly into the Atlantic Ocean. The Guarapares International Airport is the airport in the city and offers numerous flights to and from this destination. Recife, Brazil was built as a port city running along tropical, white-sand beaches dotted with palms and coral reefs running the span of the thriving coastline. The urban area is fast growing and is connected by a number of bridges and continuous waterways. In 1982, the nearby city of Olinda was declared a UNESCO World Heritage Site and brought about quite a bit more tourism to the area, which led to the discovery of Recife, by many tourists seeking relaxing holidays in tropical climates.

Recife Brazil's name was drawn from the Portugese word for reef. The area was one of the first in Brazil to be settled by the Portugese in 1534. Pernambuco prospered from the sugar cane industry, which was originally introduced to the area by a man named Duarte Coehlo. Recife Brazil had an abundance of fertile soil and an extremely suitable climate for the cultivation of cane. The indigenous people of Brazil were employed to work the land and cultivate the sugar cane in the areas fields. When that was no longer a viable solution to produce, the crop slaves from Africa were brought into the country between the 16th and 19th century to replace the unco-operative indigenous people and work the land themselves. This Brazilian state has very visible elements of black culture in food, dance and music because of the African people's influence. The combination of Indians, black slaves and Portuguese was so significant that it made Recife Brazil one of the most culturally diverse cities in the country.

During the 18th century rich farmers from the neighboring city of Olinda fought with traders from Recife Brazil Recife's harbour allowed the center clear advantage followed by victory which was a decisive factor in Recife's growth into a large and thriving city. In Recife Brazil history Recife Carnival is a long-standing tradition. Music stages are spread out downtown and throughout the city and at night the streets are filled with reverberating music and colourful, alluring costumes. Recife Brazil history has seen this custom start in December and end the day before Ash Wednesday. The Recife Carnival has a famous tradition that takes place early Saturday morning. There is a party hosted downtown drawing in as many as 1.5 million outfitted celebraters to commemorate the crack of dawn.

Any hotel Recife has will await you at this time of year with open arms, festive adornments, and feverishly charged rhythms. The streets come alive with native Indian and African Maracatu beats of Frevo and samba. No matter which hotel Recife has to offer, you will be continuously enchanted by the sights, sounds and activities Carnival presents. The unceasing hospitality of this unique Brazilian city will leave you craving more of its captivating and delightful culture.

SAO LUIS

Named after Louis XIII (of France), Sao Luis is considered one of Brazil's most beautiful cities. The city's architecture is very colonial - it was founded by a French pirate -with magnificent churches and palaces. Sao Luis is nothing short of charming and delightful fusion of all the cultures of Brazil - African, indigenous and Portuguese. This beautiful little town is well worth going out of your way to visit.

NATAL

Natal Brazil is the well-known and bustling beach capital of northern Brazil with pristine white-sand beaches stretching 9 kilometers from The Fort to the Lighthouse. A contemporary and sprawling area attracting more than one million visitors every year the Brazil Natal sunshine is as endless as the beaches seem. Natal is framed by stunning beaches and and massive sand dunes that run all along its 40 kilometer coastline. Natal is a clean, safe and friendly place for visitors and has relatively few high-rise buildings and little traffic interfering with the beautiful surrounding landscape. Geographically speaking Natal is the area is the closest point of Brazil to Europe.

Being a fairly small place, familiarity with Natal comes quickly. Visitors enjoy many activities from lazy days spent under sun-filled skies, surfing the waves of the deep blue or discovering the renowned sand dunes by dune buggy. Brazil Natal offers clarion waters and an inhabitancy of underwater reefs just offshore for those interested in discovering the wonders of aquatic life while snorkeling or diving offshore.

Natal, Brazil has two urban centers which include the cities of Natal and Ponta Negra, the latter being the more popular area for entertainment, food and accommodation. Known as the "City of Sun" and also as "The City of Dunes" Natal Brazil is located in the northeastern tip of Brazil. Lying about 15 degrees south of the equator the sun shines on for more than 3,000 hours every year and the days seem to last forever. The average temperature in Natal, Brazil is about 28 degrees celsius. During the summer season it normally reaches 38 degrees celsius with the water at a soothing 26 degrees. The majority of rain happens between March and July and luckily storms happen pretty rarely!.

When planning your Brazil Natal vacation keep in mind that the best time to visit is from November through February and then again in July. During this time several hotels become fully booked and the prices can soar for last minute guests. There are some four and five star contemporary hotels that are found in Via Costeira offering exceptional service, amenities and scenery. They are all as close as can be to the waterfront and most rooms have a lovely frontal ocean view and some have pristine private beaches to relax on. To find a wider range in accommodation visit Ponta Negra where you can find a variety of Natal Brazil hotels to suit every traveler and every budget. Going either north or south of the city there are a lot of choices for any type of Natal Brazil hotel you're looking for among the many beaches found in the area. No Natal Brazil vacation would be complete without a look around the many different beaches, bars and restaurants this Brazilian hotspot has.

When searching for the perfect Natal Brazil beach to savor your relaxing seaside vacation there are lot of options for the beach-loving tourist. The first beach north of Natal is Redinha, meaning "small net" in Portugese. Further on from Redinha there are lots of other beaches offering many different attractions from diving, action packed clubs and bars, plenty of dunes and host of seafood restaurants. You can also find many similar attractions and excitement in the string of beaches south of Natal. Of course the vibrant, warm sunshine will always be present no matter which Natal Brazil beach location you choose spend your holiday at.

FORTALEZA

Two words define Fortaleza the capital of the state of Ceará State in Brazil: Sun and Party.

The sun is absolute on 25KM of the city urban of stunning beaches; Fortaleza is the Brazilian coastal city with most sunny days throughout the year. Fortaleza is a hot city with a refreshing coastal wind to make all so pleasant, it has little variation in temperature across the year; this happens because Fortaleza is located very near the Equatorial Line. There is a slight decrease from April to August, but the temperature still remains between 24 and 28 degrees Celsius. The rest of the year you will find 30 degrees Celsius being the most common. There can be a clear concentration of rain some days in the first half of the year, but from July to January, Fortaleza sees very little rain.

Party is the permanent state of spirit of the people and the city. Forrò is the typical musical style on the region of the northeast, is on the people's blood, on the beach, on the bars, on the restaurants, in the dance clubs, on the streets of Fortaleza. Most beach bars are open until very late into the night and in some of the beach towns like Cumbuco and Canao Quebrada, well often they don't shut!

But for the serious night goers, nightclubs are plentiful, atmospheric and intense in Fortaleza. The nightlife starts to fully liven by midnight then well into the early hours to 6am – 7am. The main tourist hotspots for clubs is just of the beach of Iracema, with several nightclubs and bars based together, with clubs like Café del Mar and Mambo's being packed every night of the week playing popular dance tracks mixed perfectly to a Latin style, and the famous disco Piratas being filled on Monday nights for the Forrò music lovers. Further into the city area of Iracema at Dragao do Mar which is the main social meeting place for Brazilians alike, we have the hugely popular Armazem disco, which fills to the thousands of dance happy Brazilians, especially on Wednesdays and Saturdays, also at the Centro square they are plentiful of other bars and of cause several packed out restaurants. I do need to mention the huge Mucuripe disco, busiest night normally being Fridays it carters for all type of music lovers with 5 different music theme areas.

If people's happiness and hospitality and the cultural animation that make people love Fortaleza (see some more at the first sight, other elements also contribute to include the city, a modern capital, it has become one of the most preferred holiday destinations of Brazilian and Latin-American visitors due to the combination of a privileged nature with an excellent infra-structure, sophisticated tourist elements. Famous for the friendliness and hospitality of its people, for its animated lights and incredible cultural diversification, Fortaleza is a well developed city and possesses a modern infrastructure, harbours, international airport, and the best international hotel chains, shopping centres, theatres, bars, nightclubs, as well as ample green and leisure areas. It had been for decades being a popular destination for Brazilian tourists, but in recent years, the fame of Fortaleza has been gaining the world, and the number of Europeans, North and South Americans travellers coming to Ceará has grown fast. Located in the northeastern corner of Brazil, Ceará is the Brazilian State nearest Europe and North America. With more than 3 million people, Fortaleza is the fifth largest metropolitan area in Brazil. On top of that, it's worthy mentioning that Brazil is free from natural disasters, and is a country with low cost of living.

The seashore, running the length of the city, has a variety of attractions. The most important urban beaches of Fortaleza are Meireles, Volta da Jurema and Mucuripe, connected to each other by the Avenida Beira-Mar. Modern buildings, including first class hotels, and very many beach bars (barracas) and restaurants, which serve local cuisine and delicious seafood dishes, line this three-mile long avenue. By early evening it opens its market stalls for all its hand made goods, and is renowned for thousands of locals and tourist strolling along the stretch and watching the world go by. Praia do Futuro to the south east of the city is another very popular tourist beach due to its gorgeous white sands and relaxed atmosphere about 7 km long, is the preferred one for bathing and surfing. Praia do Futuro was made famous by its barracas (rustic restaurants built on the beach sand), which offer excellent food and local musical shows. Beach Park at Ponta das Dunas, just out of the city, has the largest water park in Brazil, and like always a fantastic beach, offering also one of the best hotel resorts in Brazil.

Cumbuco also need mentioning, it is the first stop in the Sunset Coastline, which heads west, and it holds some exciting experiences that only the beaches of Ceará can offer. Famous for its wind surf environment and facilities, local natural scenery beauty and miles of ever-changing sand dunes forms perfect for thrilling buggy rides. One of the other most famous attractions in Cumbuco is in the middle of the dunes, Banana do Lagoa, where visitors enjoy many water activities such as kayak, speedboat and banana-boat rides on the lagoon. Thanks to its attractiveness and the proximity with Fortaleza (30 minutes drive from the city), Cumbuco is one of the areas in Brazil with the greatest presence of foreigners looking for a residence. This has caused a boom in the real estate and construction sectors. Even though Cumbuco is still a small village, visitors can find a range of services in different categories and prices, among restaurants, hotels and inns.

Back to the city, Fortaleza is celebrated also for its culture and it's retain of the architectural features from the turn of the century. Some big attractions are the Estoril buildings, which houses restaurants and an exhibition gallery, the Ponte dos Ingleses (Bridge of the Englishmen) from which beautiful sunsets can be observed, and the Cultural Centro Dragão do Mar, one of the most modern and complete cultural centres in Brazil, and the Statue of Iracema, one of the landmarks of the city, is at Volta da Jurema.

Just like anywhere no city is perfect, Fortaleza of cause has many poor areas including some favelas, and some other dangerous areas within the city. Some 'service ladies' can hang around some streets, beggars will be begging in the main tourist spots, and some petty theft can occur if your not careful. The course of action is simple and obvious enough; don't wonder off the beaten track in the city any larger towns (many beach villages are generally crime free) until you are very familiar with the areas and don't flash the cash about or the gold. With that aside, you will have a fantastic time.

CURITIBA

Curitiba is a city of 1.5 million, many with European ancestry, and a major inland port for the upper Amazon River areas. The city goes back to 1669, when the first European settlement was established. Rubber plantations brought wealth to the area until the decline in the 1920s. Today, the city is known for its imports of Brazil nuts, electronic and manufacturing equipment and petroleum refining.

The emphasis in Curitiba is protecting the environment with innovative urban planning and many parks and gardens. One of the best is the Jardim Botanico garden, which includes a two-floor greenhouse shaped like a castle. The Botanical Museum within the park features an array of exotic Brazilian plants.

For a real treat, you'll want to take the narrow-gauge train that leaves Curitiba for Paranagua. Completed in 1880, it provides a breathtaking journey of three hours, traveling under 13 tunnels and over 67 bridges. The tracks cross the verdant Serra do Mar mountain ranges and traverse numerous canyons. Along the way you'll see streams, waterfalls, and vibrant vegetation.

One of the two daily trains is specifically for tourists. With comfortable cars, it stops at scenic spots. A regular train, at a much lower price, is also available. You can travel one way by train and return by bus to Curitiba or travel on to the large port of Paranagua.

FLORIANOPOLIS

Florianopolis, or Floripa as it is also known, is the capital of Santa Catarina state in the south of Brazil. It has a vibrant and colourful mix of the best Brazil has to offer and is located between the cities of Porto Alegre and Curitiba. There are 400-year-old forts, baroque churches beautiful colonial buildings and on the eastern side some of the best surfing in Brazil to be found. Situated in a rich farming expanse the city is a commercial and cultural mecca. The population in the metropolitan area of the island is home to over 821,000 people while the island itself is home to over 400,000 people. Florianopolis is connected to the mainland by a bridge which allows easy access to the rest of Brazil and it's neighboring countries.

The northern half of the island of Florianopolis is the most densely populated while the southern half remains more isolated and less developed then it's northern counterpart. More then 100 white sand beaches and their prime location draw many South Americans to Florianopolis Brazil year after year. Both international and domestic flights arrive and depart from Herciliop Luz International Airport in Florianopolis Brazil. It is roughly a one hour flight from Sao Paulo and about a 2 hour flight from Rio de Janeiro and there are also daily flights running to and from all major cities in Brazil.

With Florianopolis accommodation there is an abundance of choices between many resorts, hotels, cabanas, guesthouses and bed and breakfasts. There are even campsites for the more adventurous traveler. For a taste of luxury and arresting ocean views consider finding a suite directly on the beach. Most Florianopolis accommodation offers at least the basic amenities while some other higher end villas and hotels boast magnificent landscapes, artistically designed suites, spas and saunas, garden views and impressive on-site restaurants to flavour even the most finicky palates. There are many activites to be enjoyed on this sub-tropical island including gliding, kayaking, windsurfing kite surfing, nature hikes and more!

While relaxing seaside by your hotel Florianopolis keeps a vibrant and festive beat. Locals and tourists fill cafes and restaurants, music spills from daytime patios and markets and ocean front shops come alive with intent treasure hunters. At the Public Market in downtown, live music can be heard just about everday and see many local artists who's work is sold throughout the island.

According to frequent guests of the island, the best time to visit is between March and April when the sun blazes and the crowds are not too intense. Although the weather is great this time of year, be prepared to be amidst crowds of people when visiting local attractions or shopping and dining. The island's entrancing natural beauty, warm ocean waters, ongoing hospitality local good cheer keep visitors coming back for more year after year.

INFRASTRUCTURE

Natal São Gonçalo Airport will be the largest airport in Latin America.

Modernisation and expansion of all airports in World Cup match destinations.

Investment of US$21.7 billion in roads, railways and ports.

Brazil's successful bid to host the World Cup in 2014 will provide a huge boost to the country's tourism and project Brazil into the international limelight. Conscious that Brazil needs to address the current deficient infrastructure in some parts of this huge country, the Brazilian government has announced several ambitious investment plans for the near future.

Through the government Growth Acceleration Program, US$21.7 billion of public and private funds will be used to improve transport infrastructure including roads – these are set to receive over 75% of the investment – railways and ports.

Airports are another major focus for investment. Natal's new São Gonçalo Airport is under construction, which when completed, will be the largest in Latin America.

Airports in other cities hosting World Cup matches in 2014 such as Brasilia, Rio de Janeiro and Sao Paulo, will receive US$2.5 billion for expansion and modernisation by 2010.

The 2014 World Cup, expected to attract over 500,000 visitors, will see massive investment in infrastructure such as public services –

for example, hospitals, and new hotels – as well as stadiums in the 18 proposed match locations (including Natal) throughout the country.

ACCELERATED INFRASTRUCTURE

The "Growth Acceleration Program" (PAC) implanted by the Federal Government expands the supply of energy, transportation, housing and health to bolster the Brazilian economy during this time of recession abroad.

Brazil is experiencing an exceptional period in attracting investment. Billions of dollars are invested in various sectors of the economy, to expand transportation, energy, basic sanitation and housing infrastructure, which will ensure growth in production capacity, employment and expansion of domestic consumption.

In mining alone, investments will reach the significant milestone of US$ 40 billion. Domestic production of steel, for example, will double with the building of new steelmaking plants. The automobile industry will also experience rapid expansion: in 2008, a record 3.2 million vehicles were produced.

And, based on scheduled investments, installed capacity will reach 6 million cars by 2013, which will make Brazil the sixth largest producer of automobiles in the world. The good business environment and favorable outlook for the domestic market and exports have led productive investment in Brazil to beat all previous records in recent years. The investment rate was 17.6% of Gross Domestic Product at the end of 2007, rising to 20% in the 3rd quarter of 2008, an all time record. The government has established a target of 21% for this rate for 2012.

Boosting the economy

In the beginning of 2007, the federal government launched the "Growth Acceleration Program" (PAC) which organized and defined investments in logistics, energy, social and urban infrastructure projects, which result in direct improvements for the Brazilian people. The initial projection was an investment of US$ 220 billion from 2007 to 2010, but in February 2009 the federal government increased this amount by 26% to US$ 301 billion to be used by 2010 as an additional tool for bolstering the economy and countering the negative effects of the international financial crisis on Brazil. In addition, PAC includes another US$ 136 billion in investments that will be concluded between 2011 and 2013.

The group of investments that make up PAC are organized into three categories: Logistical Infrastructure, involving the construction and expansion of highways, railways, ports, airports and waterways; Energy Infrastructure, involving the generation and transmission of electricity, the production, exploration and shipping of petroleum, natural gas and renewable fuels; and Social and Urban Infrastructure, covering sanitation, housing, subways and urban trains. In addition to other activities, the investment plan will mean the construction, modification, duplication and recuperation, in four years, of 45,000 kilometers of highways, 2,518 kilometers of railways, the expansion and improvement of 12 ports and 20 airports, generation of more than 12,386 MW of electricity, construction of 13,826 kilometers of transmission lines, installation of four new refinery or petrochemical units, construction of 4,526 kilometers of gas pipelines and the installation of 46 new biodiesel plants and 77 ethanol plants.

The budget for the Growth Acceleration Program (PAC) for 2007 to 2010 is <u>US$ 301 billion</u>. there are <u>2,198 infrastructure projects</u> planned in the areas of transportation, energy, sanitation, housing and wa ter resources.
Source: www.pa c.gov.br

Investments in Petrobras, the state-owned oil company, are included in PAC, which will invest US$ 174.4 billion up to 2013, in the exploration of petroleum and natural gas and the construction of new refineries, among other projects. The investments carried out by PAC intend to stimulate the efficiency of the main sectors of economy, as well as to boost technological modernization, to accelerate growth in areas already in expansion and to foster growth in depressed areas, increasing competitiveness and integrating Brazil with neighboring countries and with the world.

DEMOCRACY

Democratic and institutional stability with protected democratic values and no internal conflicts, Brazil currently enjoys one of its best historical periods, with branches of government in balance.

Brazil today is a consolidated democracy based on solid institutions, with a stable political environment that guarantees individual rights. At 508 years, Brazil is a country with a high degree of institutional, political and economic maturity with immense potential for growth and investment. Today, the country is a player in the global economy, with the establishment of an intense dialogue with groups such as the G-20. After 21 years of dictatorial regimes, redemocratization took place in 1984 and was consolidated in 1988 with the enactment of a new Constitution, a milestone in the process of reducing existing social inequalities. Since then, Brazil has enjoyed a full democracy, with a system of republican controls that led to the impeachment of a President in 1992 by means of a process carried out by the legislative branch. Democratic path has prevailed in the past twenty years, with five presidential elections taking place regularly. Democracy follows its course, with no institutional interruptions. There have been episodes of intensely active political participation by the population in the country's history, such as in the national referendum on the government system held in 1993. The population had to choose their form of government, with options that ranged from presidentialism to parliamentarism, including monarchism. The people voted to maintain the presidential system. From then on, presidents of different ideological backgrounds and parties have been elected and have fully carried out their terms. Their emphasis has always been on controlling inflation, improving education, providing efficient macroeconomic management and a better business environment, and reducing social inequalities. Brazil changed its currency and inflation was stabilized in 1994. The country also allowed presidential reelection as of 1997 and continued firmly on the path of constitutionality. Public accounts are in order. The government surplus has been constant at around 4% since 2004 and the Debt/GDP ratio has been falling. Since 2007, Brazil has gone from being a debtor to becoming a creditor in the international market. In 2008, Brazilian international reserves soared to US$ 207 billion for the first time, an increase of US$ 143 billion since March 2006. A set of institutional reforms have been implemented over the past twenty years. The Law of Fiscal

Responsibility, approved in 2000, served as the basis for improved government management. The implementation of the guaranteed credit system increased the volume of loans made to companies and individuals. The creation of regulatory agencies between 1996 and 2001 ensure that privatized public services meet the needs of the population. The new Innovation Law of 2004 has boosted research and development and opened the way for universities and private companies to join in a major innovative effort.

INTERNATIONAL: OPEN MARKETS AND MULTILATERALISM

The defense of Brazilian interests is based on the understanding that the fruits of globalization need to be better divided to achieve economic development with social justice.

Brazilian foreign policy has a long tradition in the defense of peace and the search for sustainable development, emphasizing the need for peaceful solutions for disputes and the reinforcement of multilateralism. Brazil has defended a reform of the international system and its institutions in order to be more representative of the new social and economic reality and in light of the growing importance of developing countries. With this purpose, Brazil actively participates in the reform process of the United Nations and has supported the idea of increasing the number of the permanent members of the Security Council. Brazilian diplomacy has been striving at trade negotiations at the World Trade Organization (WTO) to generate effective gains for poorer countries and undo the protectionist measures in place in richer countries, especially in agriculture. The creation of the G-20, led by Brazil, has allowed developing countries to be at the center of international decisions. The Brazilian push for changes in the international order has become more urgent with the worsening of the international financial crisis during the second half of 2008. At the financial G-20, Brazil is among the countries that discuss necessary reforms and measures to overcome this situation and prevent it from recurring. Brazilian diplomacy is guided by the same objectives as the administration's domestic plan: sustainable growth aimed at reducing poverty and inequalities.

 The President   of the Republic, Luiz Inácio Lula da Silva, was one of the proponents of the International Action Against Hunger and Poverty, which received broad support from the international community.

Brazil has also been engaged in climate change debates, emphasizing sustainable development projects. The country is an example in the use of renewable energy sources ever since it was proven that biofuels contribute to the reduction of polluting emissions.

Supported by the international initiatives of the Brazilian government, Brazilian companies have accelerated their process of internationalization by increasing exports to its traditional partners and to new markets.

Sales have increased significantly to new markets in Africa, the Middle East and Asia, as well as to our partners in Latin America and the Caribbean. Sales to traditional markets, such as the

European Union and the United States, have also increased. Brazil is concerned with increasing and diversifying its purchases, especially from regional partners with whom it has surpluses. Brazilian diplomacy is directed toward the economic and social development of the continent. Globally, it is clear that Brazil has risen in stature in recent years, both domestically and internationally.

FOREIGN INVESTMENT

In recent years, Brazil has become increasingly attractive for foreign direct investment (FDI).

According to the United Nations Conference on Trade and Development (UNCTAD), during 2008, the country's inflow of FDI grew 20.6%, reaching the record figure of US$41.7 billion. In its 2009 outlook, UNCTAD said that the increase in inflows to Brazil were in sharp contrast to global FDI which fell by an estimated 10% in 2008.

UNCTAD ranks Brazil 8th among the leading targets for FDI, ahead of important economies such as Japan, Germany, Italy and India. Brazil has a large potential market, still partly untapped and its economy has expanded over the last few years, two aspects which are vital determining factors in attracting FDI.

Brazil is rich in raw materials and oil and gas are two areas that have been receiving significant investment. Major oil fields have been discovered during the last few years, the latest in the Tupi oil fields in 2008.

First extraction took place in May 2009 and the Tupi fields are estimated to amount to 33 million barrels.

Brazil is one of the world's top biofuel producers and major FDI has been made in this field. The manufacturing sector, particularly cars – Fiat recently invested US$2.8 billion in the expansion of their plant at Betim – and telecommunications are also extremely attractive markets for FDI in Brazil.

STATE CONSTITUTION

The Federative Republic of Brazil includes the Federal Government, States, Municipalities and the Federal District. The Federal Government is the federative unit itself, divided into states, subdivided into municipalities. The Federal District is a special entity that accrues the roles intended for states and municipalities and it is not subdivided. Although there is certain overlapping of the Federal Government regarding the States, the Federal District and the Municipalities, and those surrounding the latter, the Brazilian federative systemgrants financial, administrative and political autonomy to all of its entities. By defining and transferring government assets and revenues, as well as authority to carry out any concrete acts and even enact laws, including State Constitutions and Organic Laws of the Municipalities and of the Federal District, the Federal Constitution of Brazil ensures to each one of them full self-organization, selfgovernment, self-administration and self-legislation capacity.

THE JUDICIARY AND DEPARTMENT OF JUSTICE

The Brazilian legal system is based on codes. Court decisions are based on laws enacted by the Federal Government, States, Municipalities and the Federal District, in accordance with their authority levels. In case there is no provision of law applicable to the conflict, the judge shall decide based on analogy and general principles. Case law has no force of law in Brazil, but it is important assistance for the judges to make their decisions. Below, the organization and institutional commitment of the Judiciary exercised in Pernambuco, except those relating to special, election and military justices, which, although are very important in their fields, have no influence for the interest of the investor.

PRIVATE REAL ESTATE MATTERS

1 TIDE LANDS

Tide lands are located in the sea coast and in river, lake and island banks (up to the point where the influence of the tide is perceived), in a depth of 33 meters, measured horizontally to the land portion, counted from the position of the mean high water level of 1831 (art. 2 of Decree-Law No. 9.760 de 1946).

The annual variation of the mean high water level makes impossible for it to be considered as a point of reference for delimiting tide lands. Thus, the mean high water level of 1831, which is in force until now, was established. A new sea retreat land, in relation to that level of 1831, or "added tide land", a name given to the properties arising from the sea retreat will arise. Approximately 60% of the territory of Recife for example, the capital of the State of Pernambuco, is composed of tide lands. Three thousand properties are reached in the municipality. As in the case of Recife, part of the territory of the other municipalities of the State is also composed of tide lands.

Tide lands belong to the Federal Government and may be used by individuals through occupancy or fee farm, with the transfer of useful ownership (right of possession, use and enjoyment of the property, which also allows the transfer by succession or disposal) to third parties. Fee farm results from the Federal Government ownership, through an administrative proceeding in the Federal Government Heritage Department, the former Federal Government Heritage Service – SPU, imposing on the beneficiary an obligation to pay the rent on an annual basis – corresponding to 0.6% of the adjusted market value of the property. In case of disposal of the useful ownership the tenant in fee shall pay the laudemium (recognition fee) – a fee of 5% of the sale value. The occupancy of tide lands is authorized upon payment of an annual occupancy fee and does not imply recognition by the Federal Government of any property right of the occupant over the land. The Federal Government's vesting in possession of these lands may occur within 90 days when they are located in urban areas, or within 180 days when they are located in rural areas. In the disposal of the right of fee farm or occupancy of tide lands or added tide lands, in addition to the documents required for the transfer of the property ownership, it is also necessary to submit the Federal Government tax certificate and the certificate of transfer and payment of laudemium.

TAXES IMPOSED ON REAL ESTATE IN BRAZIL

The Brazilian law created three types of real estate taxes: ITBI (Property Transfer Tax), IPTU (Municipal Real Estate Tax) and ITR (Rural Land Tax).

ITBI – Property Transfer Tax

The ITBI is charged upon the transfer of property in two ways:

(i) If the transfer results from donation or inheritance it will be performed by the State where the property is located;

(ii) if the transfer results from a purchase it will be charged by the municipality where the property is located. The quantification of the ITBI value depends on the calculation basis and tax rate established by each municipality. The calculation basis is not the sale value, but rather the market value. The rate is 2% or 3% depending of the city. The time of payment of the ITBI is provided in the law of the location in which the property is located, which may occur either before or after the public deed has been recorded.

IPTU – Municipal Real Estate Tax

The IPTU is a tax imposed on urban properties of locations fitted with the basic improvements defined in the law.

Buyers shall request a tax clearance certificate from the municipal government where the property in located, since they will be responsible for paying the property tax debts, even those prior to the acquisition.

ITR – Rural Land Tax

When a rural property is acquired a certificate must be requested at the Federal Revenue Service in order to check any ITR debts, since it is essential to confirm the ITR payment for the past five (5) years in order for the public deed to be registered.

The acquirer shall submit, on annual basis, a Rural Land Tax Return ("DITR") and inform Federal Revenue Service – through the ITR Information and Record Update Document ("DIAC") – of the property acquisition.

TRADE REGISTER

For the regular exercise of a business activity the Brazilian law requires the registration with the Public Register of Business Companies of individual businesspersons and business companies organized for the production and circulation of goods and services. In addition to individual registration and organization of business companies, all alterations to the Articles of Association and Bylaws as well as the record of books and other acts specifically provided by law shall be submitted to the Public Register of Business Companies.

In order to avoid unnecessary expenses businesspersons shall consult – before any formalization – a qualified professional and the Municipal Government of the location where they intend to settle so as to check whether there is permission for developing the purpose of the intended business activity. Municipalities establish residential, commercial, industrial and combined zones in which certain developments may or may not be authorized. Investors shall only start the formal stages of the Commercial Register upon a positive response to the consultation. The other types of non-business companies, associations and entities are not subject to the Commercial Register and their Certificates of Incorporation shall be filed with Company Registers.

BUSINESS ACTIVITY

The Brazilian law allows the development of the business activity by means of Individual Businesspersons and Business Companies.

Business companies – due to the complexity of the investments required and the separation between the company's and its shareholders' equity – is the most common form.

The law provides for various corporate types for the performance of a variety of business activities. However, two types have proven to be most attractive and represent nearly 99% of the registrations with the State Trade Register: Limited Liability Companies and Corporations – they conciliate the dynamics of the corporate organization and the level of responsibility and transparency among the partners. It should be noted that some activities such as management of consortiums, insurance, bank institutions, among others, must be organized as a Corporation under the law.

Limited Liability Companies are governed by the Civil Code and organized upon execution of the articles of association by two or more partners, whether individuals or legal entities. At the time of organization their capital stock, which represents the financial investment made by the incorporators, has to be established.

The capital stock may be subscribed for and fully paid at the time of organization or only subscribed for future payment, which may be made in cash or in assets, provided that they are liable to appraisal in cash. The capital stock will be divided into shares, which will be assigned to shareholders in proportion to the investments made by each one.

As a rule, partners only answer with their personal assets up to the full payment of the capital stock. After full payment, the company will answer with its assets for the debts incurred.

However, there are exceptions to this rule, in which partners and officers may answer with their own assets, as in the case of employment relationships, debts with social security and tax debts, for acts performed by the officers or partners in violation of the Law or the articles of association.

Articles of Association: The Certificate of Incorporation of a Limited Liability Company

The Articles of Association shall contain the following elements:

a) title;

b) preamble;

c) body of the articles of association with mandatory and optional clauses;

d) closing.

The body of the articles of association contains mandatory and optional clauses.

The mandatory clauses are:

a) corporate name;

b) capital, expressed in currency, the share of each partner, payment form and term;

c) full address of the headquarters and branches, if any;

d) accurate and detailed description of the corporate purpose;

e) duration;

f) the date on which the fiscal year shall end;

g) managers and their responsibilities;

h) participation of each partner in profits and losses;

i) courts or arbitration clause.

The optional clauses are established according to the interests of the partners, for instance: a) the rules of the partners' meetings;

b) accessory application of Corporation rules; c) removal of partners for cause;

d) authorization for a non-partner to become a manager;

e) creation of an audit committee.

The closing shall establish the place, execution date, the signatories' names and signatures and the attorney's initials.

Corporations

Corporations are governed by Federal Law No. 6.404/1976. They are organized by means of public or private subscription by recording the minutes of the organization meeting or a public deed.

Corporations are also known as joint-stock companies and may be publicly-held or closely-held. In both types shares are always registered and bearer shares are prohibited. Publicly-held companies are authorized to distribute and trade their shares with the public, and prior to any trade it must be registered with the Brazilian Securities Commission (CVM). Corporate relations are governed by the Bylaws, which are approved at the time of organization. The capital stock is represented by shares and depending on the nature of the rights or advantages granted to shareholders said shares may be common, preferred, or participating. The shareholders' liability is limited to full payment of their interest in the capital stock and the possibility of answering with their own equity for the Company's debts is more limited than that found in other corporate types.

Minutes of the Organization Meeting of a Corporation

The minutes of the general organization meeting of a Corporation shall contain:

a) the place, time, month, day and year in which it was held;

b) presiding officers: full name of the chairman and secretary;

c) quorum required to hold the meeting; d) publication of notice of meeting, except in the case where all subscribers are present;

e) the agenda;

f) resolutions.

The resolutions shall govern:

a) the approval of the Bylaws;

b) the declaration of organization;

c) the election of officers and their term of office;

e) the election of the members of the Board of Directors, if any;

f) the election of the members of the Audit Committee, if permanent;

g) establishment of directors' fees.

For the organization, a deposit with a bank agency of at least 10% of the issue price of shares subscribed for in cash is required – this amount will become available to the company after evidence of its regular organization has been provided. In the case of incorporation of assets into the capital the organization meeting will appoint three experts or a specialized company in order to prepare an appraisal report on the assets incorporated.

The Bylaws shall contain:

a) the name of the corporation;

b) the duration of the corporation;

c) the address of the headquarters;

d) the corporate purpose;

e) the capital stock expressed in national currency;

f) the number of shares in which the capital stock is divided, their type (common, preferred, participating), classes of shares and whether or not they will have a par value, convertibility, and registered form;

g) duties and powers of management, form of substitution, term of office;

h) audit committee, establishing whether or not it will be permanent, with the specification of the number of members;

i) the duties of the Board of Directors, if any; and

i) the date on which the fiscal year shall end.

The partners' names and signatures as well as the attorney's initials shall be included at the end of the minutes.

PARTICIPATION OF FOREIGN INVESTOR

Foreign investors may participate in economic activities organized in Brazil basically in two ways:

(i) as a partner of a business company organized under the Brazilian laws;

(ii) opening a branch or office of a foreign company in the national territory upon authorization of the Federal Executive Branch.

The capital allocated to the operations in Brazil shall be registered by the interested party or its representative through SISBACEN (Central Bank Information System).

Participation in Companies Organized under the Brazilian Laws.

Limited Liability Companies and Corporations have the same legal rule as to the participation of foreigners in their corporate structures, as set forth in Normative Ruling No. 76/1998 from the Brazilian Trade Register Department – DNRC.

In the case of foreign individuals who are part of the corporate structure of a domestic business company, their identification shall specify:

a) name;

b) nationality;

c) marital status;

d) date of birth, if single;

e) occupation;

f) address;

g) identification document specifying the issuing body; and h) registration number with the Individual Taxpayer Registry ("CPF"). Foreign partners domiciled abroad shall appoint a representative in Brazil by a public power of attorney with powers to receive service of process in legal actions related to the company. All foreign documents shall be certified by the local notary office and initialled by the Brazilian Consulate in the country of origin and accompanied by an official translation.

The articles of incorporation of the company – if a foreign company participates therein – shall be accompanied by the following documents:

a) a document supporting the foreign company's legal existence and legitimate representation therefor;

b) a copy of the articles of association or bylaws of the foreign company;

c) a power of attorney appointing a representative in Brazil with powers to receive service of process;

d) an official translation of the documents into Portuguese by a translator registered with any Board of Trade.

Foreigners may only fill a management position at the company or be a member of the Audit Committee if they have a permanent visa to reside in Brazil and do not fall within the cases of disqualification to fill a management position; otherwise, the company shall be managed or conducted by a manager residing in Brazil.

Finally, subject to the specific formalities, the law restricts or prohibits the direct or indirect participation of foreign people in certain

activities. The participation of foreigners in health assistance activities is prohibited. The participation in the following activities is restricted:

(i) in coastal shipping companies;

(ii) an interest greater than thirty percent (30%) in news, broadcasting and audiovisual companies;

(iii) cable TV service companies; (iv) mining and hydraulic power companies;

(v) road cargo transport companies; and

(vi) airline companies.

Regarding rural activities, there are currently restrictions in the borders with other countries, that is the case of the States that does have internationalborders.

Opening of Branches by Foreign Companies

Foreign companies may only perform business activities in Brazil by means of a branch or an office upon authorization of the Federal Executive Branch, subject to the formalities set forth in Normative Ruling No. 81/1999 of DNRC.

Thus, foreign companies shall file an application with the DNRC, addressed to the Ministry of Development, Industry and Commerce, which will analyze it, without prejudice to the jurisdiction of other federal bodies, depending on the activity to be performed.

At the time of application the law requires that the following documents be submitted:

a) resolution on the branch installation in Brazil specifying the activity to be performed;

b) articles of association or bylaws;

c) list of partners, if possible;

d) evidence that the foreign company has been organized under the laws of the country of origin;

e) resolution on the representative in Brazil, with a power of attorney granting management powers and powers to receive service of process;

f) a declaration by the representative in Brazil that he or she accepts the conditions under which the Federal Government has granted the authorization for installation and operation;

g) last balance sheet; and

h) payment of service fee. The documents shall be certified by the Brazilian consulate and accompanied by an official translation.

Once the authorization for installation and operation has been granted by the Federal Executive Branch, the foreign company shall submit the following to the Board of Trade:

a) the page of the Diário Oficial da União (Official Government Gazette) that published the authorization decree;

b) the application to the Federal Executive Branch;

c) the deposit in cash of the amount of capital allocated to the Brazilian operations;

d) the address of the establishment.

In order to be effective in the Brazilian territory subsequent alterations will also be subject to the previous authorization of the Federal Executive Branch (Ministry of Development, Industry and Commerce).

TAXPAYER REGISTRATIONS AND OPERATION PERMITS

Once the company's Certificate of Incorporation has been filed, the JUNTA COMERCIAL will provide a Company Register Identification Number – NIRE, and therefore the company will be formally organized. However, the trade register itself does not make the company qualified to start its activities.

The next stages consist in registering the legal entity with the Federal Revenue Service (mandatorily) and with the State and Local Treasury Departments if it is a taxpayer thereof, and obtaining operation permits from the relevant public authorities.

The registration with the Federal Revenue Service occurs upon registration with the Brazilian Roll of Legal Entities (CNPJ) by registering with the service "Expresso Empresa" (Company Express) of the JUNTA COMERCIAL.

Once this stage has been completed, the CNPJ number will be issued and the company may obtain the state or municipal registration with the Treasury Department of the State or the respective Municipality.

The state registration will only be required for business companies that perform activities on which the ICMS is imposed. Business companies whose activities are not included in the ICMS jurisdiction must obtain a registration with the Municipal Treasury Department and will be subject to the ISS (Service Tax).

After the trade register, the company registration as a taxpayer with the Federal, State and/or Municipal Revenue Service, the company shall obtain the municipal permits required to perform the intended activity.

Businesspersons shall go to the Municipal Government in order to request an operation permit for the establishment, which permit is a document that allows establishments to operate subject to the rules as to the opening hours, zoning, building, sanitary hygiene, public safety, occupational hygiene, and environment.

A certificate of compliance from the Military Fire Department of the State shall also be obtained upon submission of the relevant documents and inspection in the establishment.

Finally, it should be noted that some activities will require authorization from the Municipal Health Surveillance Department, such as:

a) production, marketing and supply of food;

b)accommodation;

c) nursery and child day care centers;

d) health services;

e) opticians;

f) medical, dental, medical/veterinarian, nutritionist and psychologist offices;

g) pharmacies;

i) fitness, beauty and massage centers and saunas;

j) barbershops and beauty salons;

k) marketing and distribution of cosmetics and perfumery;

l)agricultural/veterinarian products;

m) sanitary hygiene products, and

n) chemical products.

Once the aforementioned permits have been obtained, the business company will be entitled to freely perform the intended activity.

REGISTRATION OF TRADEMARK AND DOMAIN NAME

The trademark registration is submitted to the Brazilian Institute of Industrial Property – INPI, a federal instrumentality associated to the Ministry of Development, Industry and Foreign Trade, also responsible for the registration of patents, technology transfer agreements, business franchise agreements, etc.

Although it is not mandatory, the registered trademark grants its holder the right of exclusive use throughout the Brazilian territory in its business industry. The registration process is performed by means of an electronic application form on INPI's website (www.inpi.gov.br), and it may be made by the interested party or an attorney.

In order to register an Internet domain name an application should be submitted to the Brazilian Internet Management Committee – CGI-Br. The registration will be granted to the first applicant that meets the formal requirements. All domain names on the Internet with the ".br" extension are registered at www.registro.br. In order for a foreign company to register a ".br" domain it shall have a legally qualified proxy in the country and a registration with the ".br" register system. Information on the registration for foreign companies may be obtained at

http://registro.br/info/regestrangeiros.html.

RETURN ON INVESTMENT (ROI)

- Investing in 365 sunny days per year
- Buying property in Brazil is as safe as buying property in Europe
- The entire north eastern region is known worldwide for its appeal and has already attracted tourists from Spain, Portugal, Italy, France, Holland, Sweden, Norway, Denmark, Finland, Germany, USA, Japan, Switzerland, England, Argentina and recently also the eastern European countries and India, as well as a huge market share of the domestic tourism market.
- Many golf courses and luxurious resorts are under construction in the State of Rio Grande Do Grande in order to attract elite tourism.

  Some examples:
  - Lagoa do Coelho Resort
  - Palmeira Golf Resort
  - Cabo de Sào Roque Resort
  - Jacumà Beach Resort
  - Grand Natal Golf
  - Portal do Brasil Resorts
- The opening of the new airport in the northern zone of Natal, will increase the number of tourists looking for high level solutions.
- The amount of tourists that have visited Brazil has increased by 50% between 2002 and 2005.

WHY BUY NOW

In the past 5 years the real estate market has seen annual increases of 20% which is a market trend that is expected to last for the next 8 years.

The real estate market in Natal is still very young and it's this element that makes it advantageous for investors that will invest before the trend could reverse.

NATAL: A RESORT FOR THE FUTURE

- Following in the footsteps of the national government, the local government has been even tougher in promoting and supporting new actions in terms of tourism and the area took part in the creation of many new infrastructure projects and tourist locations.
- The actual airport of Natal (Severo Ochoia) is situated 35 min from the larger resorts. The new airport "Sao Gonzalo Do Amarante", is designed to be the biggest commercial airport in Latin America. The airport will be the largest HUB of the whole of South America and will affirm Natal as the first tourist destination in Brazil.

- In the next 5 years more than 1.8 billion dollars will be invested in the creation of new hotels, golf courses and resorts, just in the area of Natal – Rio Grande do Norte.
- The new bridge of Natal (The Ponte de Todos-Newton Navarro), opened at the end of 2007, and has been built with the intention of connecting Natal with the beaches of Redinha and eventually with all the northern area beaches, it has replaced the old less efficient ferry-boat transportation service. This huge new infrastructure project has brought Natal 10km closer to the beaches of the northern zone.
- Domestic tourism is even more relevant in the North east of Brazil. In January of 2005 Natal received 197 domestic flights, more than 6 per day and in one year, more than 1.7 million of Brazilian tourists visit Rio Grande Do Norte from other states.
  - Natal is the closest place to Europe
  - It takes just 7 hours flying
  - Situated in the north east of Brazil
  - Mild climate all the year with an average temperature of 27°C turned perfect by a light constant breeze.
  - It will host the eighth airport of the world, "San Gonzalo" airport.
  - Great potential for market growth.

SECONDARY MARKET

Brazil's international property market is currently led by the Portuguese (27%) followed by the British (15%) and Spanish and Italians (12% each).

A fundamental factor behind the growing Brazilian property market is the ever-increasing wealth among Brazilians. Brazil's middle class represented 52% of the population in 2008 and the country's millionaire population recently almost doubled, one of the highest increases in the world.

The growing number of households with sufficient wealth to enter the property market (both first and second home markets) adds to the resale market potential. With Brazilian interest rates down to an all-time low and lending rules relaxed, the country's emerging middle class will lead increased demand. In Brazil demand is currently extremely high – Reuters Real Estate analysts put the shortfall figure at over a staggering 27 million properties over the next 15 years.

With properties situated in developments in beach resorts in the Natal area seeing rental yields of around 10% a year, the rental market presents good potential in many areas of Brazil including the major cities and resort areas such as those on the Natal coastline. Rising tourism (mainly domestic but increasingly international) has led to demand for quality short-term rental accommodation, with

Brazil's newly-affluent population keen on luxury holiday accommodation in beach resorts, particularly in the north east region.

MORTGAGE MARKET

The Brazilian mortgage market is still in its infancy, but the housing market received an enormous boost in 2008 with the introduction of mortgages for Brazilian nationals. Brazilians have traditionally bought homes with cash because of very high interest rates, but now rates have been significantly reduced – the latest rate cut was in April 2009, when it was lowered to 10.25% - mortgages are more affordable and demand is likely to increase. Mortgages are slowly becoming more available for non-residents through some banks and once this market develops it is thought that it will substantially open up the property market.

However, although the Brazilian mortgage market is small, it is growing fast. Brazil's Central Bank reported a 37% year-on-year increase in mortgage loans from February 2008 to 2009. Increasing demand from domestic buyers is boosting the mortgage market and by extension, the property market.

Brazilian banks are continually introducing new mortgage products for Brazilians and lending terms are becoming more flexible.

However, according to Forbes, the term 'subprime' is virtually unheard of in Brazil because of strict government mortgage regulations.

MARKET RISKS

Property investment into emerging markets may carry some degree of risk. However, the degree that market risk in a particular country affects a property investment depends largely on thorough due diligence conducted prior and during the purchase process.

Although Brazil presents few problems for foreign investors, it currently has one of the world's least equal societies with a huge gap between rich and poor.

However, the government is actively working to address the problem with a public housing programme which will allocate US$15 billion in the next two years to build one million houses for the poor.

Inflation used to be a perennial problem in Brazil but the government's inflation-curbing measures have kept it under control and figures in April 2009 are consistent with their target of 4.5% for the whole of 2009. Brazil has not entirely escaped the effects of the global economic downturn, although the signs are that it will recover faster than many countries because it is not burdened by debt.

According to The Economist, "the solid financial position of the government and state banks will support countercyclical measures that will mitigate the impact of the global recession."

BUYING A PROPERTY IN BRAZIL

- **Purchase of properties by foreigners**

There aren't any restrictions for foreigners buying residential or commercial real estates and Brazilian authorities encourage foreigner investments. There are however some restrictions related to specific areas such as navy properties, islands, rural areas and marshlands.

- **Lands' register**

Properties are registered in Brazil trough a public notary, under juridical supervision. Each property can be registered with just one registration number that identifies the history of the whole transaction and the physical recognition of each owner. This information can be verified by anyone which is why many Brazilians buy and sell properties without the aid of a lawyer or of a consultant, however it's strongly recommended for foreigners to buy properties with the aid of a qualified consultant.

- **Real estate assistance**

We advise anyone that intends to buy a property in Brazil to apply for a qualified real estate consultant.

Useful information

The first thing to do before buying a property in Brazil is to get an identification number called CPF. We can advise and support you through the steps to get your CPF.

Brazilian CPF

CPF is the Brazilian equivalent of a national insurance number or a social security number and can be obtained fairly simply. This number is also a legal requirement as it enables the property buyer to be uniquely identified for taxation and title purposes. Generally they are 2 methods of obtaining a CPF.

1. In person, in Brazil is the easiest and fastest way. In either a 'Corrieos' office or the Bank of Brazil you can make the application for the CPF with just your passport and pay a processing fee of just R$5.50. This application is then processed to the Receita Federal and normally just 2 days later you can go to the Receita Federal office in person with your identification to be issued you with your CPF number. Your CPF card will also later be needed to be delivered to an address in Brazil which needs to be given when making the application, your lawyers address or an agent's address is normally done for ease.

2. Make the application for a CPF number from your own residential country, via the Brazilian Consulate in that country. You will need a small processing fee (currently 4 pounds in the UK) to be paid by postal order to the consulate and the process takes approx 2 months. To make the application you can download the application form http://www.receita.fazenda.gov.br/Aplicacoes/ATCTA/CpfEstrangeiro/fcpfIng.asp . With this form completed and a copy, you can go in person or post your passport and a photo copy of your passport to the address of your nearest Brazilian consulate in your own residential country.

Legal Assistance

Many Brazilians here do not use lawyers when purchasing property in Brazil. They do this because as they are Brazilian residents, they have certain protection when using a CRECI registered real estate companies, who are certified to know the buying process in Brazil. So many Brazilian prefer to save on those extra legal costs by not hiring a lawyer for their purchase. But as a foreigner you do not have those same protections by using a certified real estate company and so would be open to many dangers as a far away investor, especially if you cannot speak the Portuguese language.

Due to this we advise that you to use a trusted lawyer when purchasing property in Brazil as the same as you would when purchasing property in Europe or North America. From our experience we know that it is important to choose a lawyer that is totally independent from the seller or developer, who will ensure only your interests are protected. I also recommend that you use a Brazilian Lawyer who is registered with the OAB (Ordem Dos Advogados Do Brasil) which is the equivalent to the Bar in the UK and of course who is fluent in your language so that you fully understand all the legalities and proceedings.

Your lawyer, as well as a good agent also, will carry out all necessary checks on the property or land in Brazil and fulfill the legal requirements of the purchase.

A good lawyer service will include:

- Check the current owners have the correct title to the property
- Check for any charges and liabilities still owed on the property
- Check your contract and advise you on the obligations for both parties
- Help you through the payment/funds transfer
- Ensure the property is registered in your name

Property Brazil Registration

The Brazilian authorities encourage foreign investment, as such there are no major restrictions for foreigners to buy and sell residential or commercial property in Brazil. Brazil is perhaps one of the few emerging markets that allow's foreign buyers to own both land and property in their own names on a 100 per cent freehold basis – making the buying process relatively straightforward.

The property registry system in Brazil is well developed and safe. Brazil real estate registration is carried out by private notary publics, under justice control. If you are buying a home that was built after 1973 it should come with a legal document know as a Matrícula. This document lists a detailed property description, all previous owners, the boundary details, any outstanding debts and all legal, financial and judicial transactions relating to the property. All land and property is registered at one single registry, and access to all information of a property is public. It is obviously very important to ensure that any land or property you buy has a clear title and your lawyer as well as a good agent also will ensure this is the case.

Payment for Brazil real estate

A sales contract is prepared by the selling broker and contains all required information of the buyer and the seller, location and specifications of the Brazil real estate and the conditions of the payment. The contract is then signed by both parties, or in the case of a notarized copy of the buyers passport and a Power Of Attorney being given by the buyer, another person can sign the contract on the behalf of the buyer. A down payment deposit (anything between 10% and 30%) is then normally paid to the seller to prevent the property from being sold to anyone else.

The taxes and registration fees (between 4.5% and 10% of the agreed declared purchase value) are also sent by the buyer to either the lawyer or acting agent. From this point the agent will arrange and pay the registration of the property into the authenticated buyers name via cartorio, in which can take up to a few weeks. All taxes are paid also in during this time. Here is the breakdown of all fees;

- Property transfer fees (ITBI) is 2% - 3% of the purchase value declared (payable at the City Hall)

- The Public Deed and notary fees usually come between 1% - 1.5% of the purchase value declared

- The land registry (The Matricula) is 2% of the purchase declared value

- Legal fees are typically 1% - 2% of the purchase price, which can depend on the value of the property.

- An extra Marine tax can be due if a front line beach, between 2% - 5% of the purchase value declared.

- There is an annual property tax (IPTU) of approximately 0.6% per year of the assessed value

With the registry completed and taxes paid, the full payment will need to be achieved by the buyer in the conditions of the authenticated contract. It will be held by the receiving bank in Brazil (automatically been registered by the central bank as all international movements of over R$10,000), the receiving bank by law will then only release the money to the sellers account when the contact and change of title has been proved.

Money Transfers for Brazil real estate

It is imperative when buying Brazil real estate that the funds are sent directly from your own bank account to the seller's bank account in Brazil, so this been registered with the Central Bank of Brazil who will provide an official receipt of funds into the country. The seller is then required to present the purchase agreement contract to the Bank to release the funds.

This also enables that the government has recorded your investment into the country to ensure that there are no problems if/when transferring funds out of Brazil if you later sell your property in the future. There are generally no limitations to returning funds overseas provided they were originally registered with the Central Bank at the time of purchase.

Your bank will not be able to offer an exchange rate at the time of transfer as the money is crystallized when it reaches Brazil (approx 5 days transfer time).

Capital Gains Tax

If you come to sell your property in Brazil, then Capital Gains tax is generally set at 15% for both Brazilians and foreigners. If you have bought your property in your personal name (rather than in a company name) then they are tax advantages that you can take advantage of!

1. You are exempt from the gain on disposal of capital earned, if it is the only property that the owner has, for sale whose value is up to R$ 440,000 provided they have not done any other alienation of property in the past five years.

   (Law No. 9,250, 1995, art. 23, RIR/1999, art. 39, III; IN SRF No 84, 2001, art. 29, I)

2. Regardless of when you sell or the amount of sale, if you reinvest in property within 6 months, the full amount can be claimed back on all of your capital gains tax from your previous

sale. If you reinvest within the 6months but under your previous declared sale price then you can claim back some of your capital gains tax as it would be offset against your new investment

3. You can also claim back 4% a year on you're declared purchased value for de-appreciation for every year you have owned the property against any capital gains tax.

4. Property improvements and furnishing (if sold with furnished in a sales contract) receipts can be also off-set against capital gains.

PERMANENT VISA

There are different kinds of VISAS for foreigners that want to buy a property in Brazil and/or live there. We believe that our clients will be interested above all in two of these categories:

1. PERMANENT VISA 1C for retired people over 50.
2. PERMANENT VISA 2A for investors

1C – Retired people over than 50

Retired people can obtain a permanent visa by proving that they benefit from a monthly income of at least $2000 or proving that they can transfer at least $2000 monthly for their whole life, the amount is valid for one person plus two dependents. The following documents must be authenticated.

- Extract of birth and marriage (if necessary) certificates.

- Copy of passport.

- Proof of residence (of the last 12 months).

- Non-criminal record.

- Proofs for dependents (if necessary).

OBS. All the documents must be officially translated and authenticated by the Brazilian Consulate.

Those that have a permanent visa in Brazil are free of charges from the Brazilian customs for importing personal property and funds that are required for accomplishing their assets. The Consulate retains the right of requiring more documents.

2A – VISA FOR INVESTORS

In adopted circumstances it is possible to obtain a permanent visa. The applicants need to apply directly to the Ministry of Labour in Brazil or consult one of their regional offices.

Brazilian Investment Visa

If a real estate agent or a developer tells you that if you buy their property in Brazil that is purchased priced higher than a value of $50,000USD and that you will qualify for a 5year investment permanent visa, then they are simply lying to you or very much misinformed!

The minimum investment value was actually revised and increased to a value now in the Brazilian Reais of R$150,000 in February 2009, and with the addition of a review of your investment after only

3 years rather than the previous 5 years. But in any case you CANNOT, and never could simply buy a property over a minimal value and then qualify for an investment visa. Many have being misled by this fact in the past.

Let us explain how you can qualify for the investment Visa in Brazil. First of all you need to open a limited business with a business account or invest into an existing company. To open a new company this process often takes about 20 days and an accountant can do this for you for around R$600, although a Lawyer will charge a lot more for this service. For a limited (Ltda) company it is required to have a minimum of 2 partners, which can be of any percentage i.e. 99.5% - 0.5%. The chosen partner does NOT need to be a Brazilian which many people seem to believe (including some Lawyers in Brazil). What is required though, where much of the confusion comes from, is the need of a business administrator who is Brazilian or a foreigner holding a RNE (someone who is a permanent resident), to administrate the company until you the owner receives the permanent visa (then have the RNE). You can then take over the full administration of the company yourself.

This bit is even more important, you need to really TRUST your chosen administrator! The administrator will automatically have powers and access to your bank account. Things that you can do, to help your case is to initiate a authenticated contract to put certain restrictions on your chosen administrator, so that it would be crime for the administrator to withdraw money from the account. This would not prevent a administrator having access to the business account, but if the administrator did steal money from the business account at least the law would be on your side. You can also make the administrator temporary so that you would administrate your own company after residency had being gained.

With your new company and business account open and ready, you can then

1. Invest a minimum of R$150,000 into your company from your own personal foreign bank account.

2. Invest a minimum of R$150,000 into an existing company. If taking this route please take extensive due diligence into the company as many may have hidden personal debts onto the company.

3. You can invest less than the minimum R$150,000 and still qualify for a investment permanent visa, but with this option you need to convince with a in depth business plan to the Ministry of Labor & Employment and the Council of Immigration on how you are going to produce a minimum of 10 new jobs for local Brazilians and how your company would effect the local economy. You will then later need to keep proofing on how you are achieving or achieved this requirement. This option is by far the most difficult to obtain.

With your money invested into a business you can then apply to the Nation Council of Immigration for your visa. A Lawyer will do this for you for around R$3,000 to R$6,000 or a full package of first opening a business for you for around R$5,000 to R$10,000. Applying for the visa to gaining the approval can take 2-4 months.

Your business, depending on what type of activity your business was registered to trade in, can then buy property. But be warned; (i) for the first 3 years your company can be under review at any time causing your visa not to be renewed after the 3 year period. It comes to the Department of the Federal Police to review, who can make steps on the spot, for establishing the physical existence of the company and the activities that it is acting. (ii) Property that is company owned (by business tax registration CNPJ) does not have the Capital Gains advantages of which could be taken of a property that is in a normal personal ownership (CPF), and the company ownership will have other taxes to pay on selling Brazil real estate depending on which tax strategy was taken for the business activity.

Summarizing Permanent Visas for investments can be issued to those that invest at least R$150.000 (REAIS).

The preconditions for this visa are:

- Copies of passports

- Non – criminal records

- Vaccination certificate (if necessary)

- Consular Tax

The ministry will verify the legalization of the application forms, the validity of Brazilians' workplaces, the kind of activity etc. The details of the procedure for this kind of visa can be supplied directly by the Ministry:

Ministerio de Trabalho e Emprego

Tel: 0055 61 317 6417

Fax: 0055 61 321 0652

All documents have to be officially translated and authenticated.

The details mentioned above are subject to change.

WHAT TO DO AND... NOT TO DO!

- You should always take a copy of your passport with you and this needs to be authenticated at the notary office (otherwise it wouldn't be valid) so that it can be shown to the authorities if required.

- You should always comply with a lawyer's or with a qualified real estate agent's advise in verifying the documents required to buy estates.

- Always apply for a real estate agent to attend your sales.

- Look around the areas where you want to buy. Try to visit personally the properties or locations and ask for the advice of a European qualified real estate agent who knows personally the properties and /or the enterprises.

- If you think about transferring your money back to Italy in the future, the best thing to do is to record your payments at the Brazilian Central Bank so that it will be easier proving where your money comes from when you will send it back to Italy.

- As buyers, look for a real estate agency with Italian and Portuguese speaking staff that live in Brazil, a European agent that attends to your investment right on the spot will save you time, money and stress.

- As with every real estate market in the world, location is the key. Find a real estate agent that knows the market well and that can help you in choosing the location and the property and negotiating the best price.

- Be clear as much as you can about the reasons of your purchase: vacation, retirement, lifestyle, business, investment etc....

...NOT TO DO!

- Brazil isn't a country for improvisation! Don't even think about it, check everything over and over! Money for qualified lawyers', accountants' and real estate agents' fees are your best investment!

- Don't believe in anything that's not written down, that hasn't been previously checked by a real estate agent, by a good lawyer and speak with a good accountant to get detailed information about taxes and about managing the transfers.

- Apply for the advice of professionals that already have a considerable experience with foreigners and with clear proven references. Always consult more than one professional before choosing the best for you.

- Be aware of anyone that could offer you <u>an assured income</u>: it's impossible to guarantee it.

- If you open a society don't give any percentage, not even 1% to a Brazilian, it isn't true that according to the laws you have to have a Brazilian associate: <u>it's a lie.</u>

- If you need a manager to open a society, hire a foreigner that is resident in Brazil and as soon as you obtain a Permanent Visa, designate yourself as the manager of the company discharging the first one.

- Don't trust those that offer to manage your company for free. Establish contractually a salary in order to keep the whole process transparent.

- If you want to start a real estate company don't give any percentage of your company to a real estate agent with CRECI, it isn't true that according to the law you have to give him a percentage: <u>it's a lie!</u>

- If you don't have a CRECI number to work as real estate agents hire an agent that has it as a technician like any technical employee.

- Don't give any percentage of your rural area (fazenda, site, granja et.) to a Brazilian just because someone tells you that it's required by law. It's a lie! A foreigner can be the owner of rural areas in Brazil unless they're situated in marshlands or they are bigger than 100 hectares.

- Never buy real estate if you haven't previously verified what you are allowed to do or not, according to the environmental authorities and verify if you are dealing with green areas/protected areas/parks/dunes etc…

- If you are thinking about buying land, first verify the City Plan.

- Don't take into account topographies unless they are "GPS topographies". If the area you're dealing with doesn't have one it's important applying for a professional to make one in order to be able to verify the correct measurements of the area and the location.

- Don't believe in stories of unique opportunities due to extraordinary situations such as health problems of a family member, disastrous financial situations, or the existence of a potential buyer close to making the deal, etc... Take your time and verify carefully what's needed, there are always good opportunities and sometimes the best investment is the one that you don't make!

- According to the Brazilian laws after two years of cohabitation with a Brazilian partner he/she acquires the same rights, as if you were married. Don't underestimate this law...!

- In Brazil there isn't a real and complete division of properties, don't underestimate this aspect...!

THE ROUGH TRUTH

- In Brazil a little restaurant/kiosk/pub/pizzeria, on the beach or not, isn't a good deal. It's a loss of time and money, it causes a lot of stress, requires a lot of bureaucracy and discussions/misunderstandings/blackmails with Brazilian staff,

- In Brazil opening lodgings is a good deal only if you can mathematically guarantee the occupancy through some contacts in Italy (tour operator, travel agency, etc.). Out of these conditions it would occur the same situation such as the little restaurant/kiosk/pub/pizzeria one.

AS USUAL THE COMMON SENSE IS ALWAYS THE BEST CHOICE!

HOW TO MAKE A GREAT BRAZILIAN INVESTMENT

To make a great Brazil Investment does need some good thought. For what it's worth, here is an insight to our own personal logic that we have used to make our Brazil investment's and what we have learnt over the years.

1. Cheap land Brazil investment that seems 'very cheap' or 'too good of a deal' is normally a sign as not a good investment. Reason for very low investment prices in Brazil, is normally because it's in the middle of nowhere. A property in near-isolation is never going to be a good investment!

   We know Brazil is a large country and it has a mammoth 7,400km of coastline to match, so it is easy to end up with near-isolation. Where's the nearest shop, bar, restaurant? If you cannot answer that question then how are you going to sell your property on to a subsequent end-user?

   A good rule of thumb is that if Brazilians have bought in the area, then it has something going for it, for this is a nation with famously good taste. Property in popular towns with laws protecting them from overdevelopment are the most lucrative option, beachfront or not, particularly if there are plenty of local activities to attract and occupy the tourists.

2. When looking for a great future Brazil investment in up and coming growing areas, it is important to look at the whole geography location of the town. For example;

What is the neighboring town like? If it is already very popular and a more expensive area, then there's a great chance that its success will 'ripple' into the next town.

Does the town have abundance in land space? If it does then the value investment growth will be slower due to higher supply. Many towns in Cearà have less limited space than others due to protected dunes or lagoons for example. This can then create lower supply and higher demand resulting in higher investment value.

Is the town clear of poverty and crime? If the answer is no, then the town will restricted to grow to any great value for many years to come.

3. Many developers and certainly most real estate companies (some knowingly but most Not knowingly) have much misleading marketing material for their developments/properties etc. Most common are;

Distances, a true 2 hour drive to the city is often written as a 1 hour drive.

Where a stroll to the beach is written is often a 2KM hike to the ocean.

Where 'our team of lawyers have done strict due diligence' is written, often just simply means that they can legally sell what they are selling.

'The Land has full building planning to build your chosen house'! This is also a crazy statement to make. 'The town hall has ear marked a section of land for building' is how the statement should be written, IF the town hall passes the land to be sectioned into 'quadra's' and 'lotes'. But to get an actual building permit to build a house, an actual house design with full details needs to be applied for. To gain a building permit also takes a cost and patience. So how can the land have a building permit before someone has bought the individual land plot, the land plot being registered, the new owner has even chosen a house design to apply for!

4. One of the more worrying Brazil investment products that are getting more common, that normally go together with our pointers on number 1 and 3, are developers that buy huge portions of land very very cheap. So cheap because its miles away from anyway without any infrastructure in place.

Developers can buy this type of huge areas for somewhere near just R$2 per meter square, then they go into the process to sub divide the land into 100's of small land plots of say 450M2 (just big enough to build a house on). The developers will then sell these small land divisions to unsuspecting buyers for huge profits at prices per meter square, near to price rates that are sold for land that is in developed popular areas much nearer to the city.

The developer will also often state that they are building infrastructure, right next to where the land plots for sale are, a hotel or/and a leisure center with shops etc etc. This to convince you that the already over priced plots are going to hugely increase in value, to make an excellent investment.

The basics of a good investment, is simply 'supply and demand' no matter how beautiful the area may be. A hundred hugely over priced small land plots all for sale in the middle of nowhere is never going to be a wise investment.

5. Has your chosen estate agent ever been to Brazil or are they simply regurgitating a mixture of the developer's marketing material and Wikipedia? Be very wary of this. Many Overseas real estate company's simply have very good sales pitches and techniques to wheel in the client. Most have never even being to Brazil and definitely do not know what they are

actually trying to sell to you.

It's much better for you, the customer, if your agent actually knows the areas so can cast a critical eye over the location and qualities and is able to offer their considered opinion. Your estate agent is there for advice, guidance and information and should have thorough product knowledge. You are entitled to have sight of all information such as licenses, contracts, plans and so on, and any documentation issues.

6. Are huge multi giant developments a good idea for your Brazil investment ? To our mind, we think not. When we was first scouting Brazil for investment potentials in 2001 and 2002 we looked into many of these giant developments in the North East of Brazil. Many of these huge developments (by foreign developers) are still not built now. Some had folded even after taking peoples deposits and some are still years behind with the investors of these apartments etc.... still without a property never mind an investment.

It is clear to see now that so many of these foreign developers just totally under estimated just how long and difficult it would be to gain ALL the licenses required. To gain town hall approvals is one thing, which is a point where many developers wrongly start to try to sell their developments, but to gain all environmental licenses is completely another aspect, which can certainly take years to gain and can take many redesigns of the project before being granted.

The bigger the development the harder the environmental licenses are to obtain. Brazil is just very strict on what is built on its beautiful coastlines, and rightly so.

7. We have two main logic thoughts when we think about large developments as an investment;

(i) Would a Brazilian want to buy one, would a Brazilian want to live in seemingly holiday complex full of foreigners. The reason I think this is because the sell on investment is much more difficult if can only sell on to another foreigner, this being only 3% of the market. It is obviously better to sell in a market that can attract 100% of the market, both the Brazilian internal market and in a area that is also attractive to foreigners.

(ii) Again, simple supply and demand. Having many properties for sale in the same development does not bear well for an investment. With this being a more likely case in a huge development bought by many as foreign investors.

8. So if buying into off-plan developments, we certainly believe it to have a safer investment potential if in a smaller development. But still be very cautious, you are still buying

something that you cannot see exactly what you are buying because you cannot see the finished article.

Off plan photo impressions can be misleading, will the finished product be as good, what standard will the materials be, does the developer have a track record, will it even be built etc etc.

9. If buying off-plan, DEFINITELY use an independent lawyer that practices in the same state in which you are buying. Ensure that:

(a) Completion dates, when the property will be registered into your name, quality finer details and advertised equipment/services are clearly written in the purchase contract.

(b) Contracts need to be written in both English (or your natural language, so you can fully understand it) and in Portuguese. IMPORTANT, a contract needs to be written in Portuguese for it to be law binding in Brazil, make sure that the contract signed by the developer is authenticated in Brazil !

(c) Your money going into Brazil direct from YOUR bank account. Funds transferred to Brazil will be automatically registered by the Banco Central to conform with money laundering regulations. This paper trail is important when it comes to reselling and getting your money back out, and will be much smoother if needing the Brazilian law to claim a refund due to developers faulting contracts etc.

10.   Are you paying over the odds for an off-plan development? How does it compare with a like for like resale house or apartment? To our opinion an off-plan developments should be at least 20% lower than a resale, because of the risk factors and because you cannot live in it or rent it for whatever years. For much of our findings we found many off-plans that are targeted to foreigner buyers can be about 20% higher than a similar resale.

11.   And now in hind sight, many developments that have being completed, the investors are struggling to 'flip' their property investment for a worthwhile profit as they had already paid over the odds of a true market value.

12.   Is a guaranteed rental deal with the developer worth it? Is the 'guaranteed' rent gross or net of condo fees, bills and even commissions? How long is the income guaranteed for? How much private use of your property does the rental contract entitle you to? Is the 'guaranteed rental' actually funded by you as you've paid an artificially inflated purchase price?

Read rental contracts carefully and do your research. Better to invest in an area with an active rental market or great facilities to attract tourists, then, whether the rental is guaranteed or not, you stand to make good money regardless.

13. You also need to be wary of many resale properties. Even though you have an advantage that you can see exactly what you are buying, can use the property to live in or rent straight away and can be much cheaper, many resale properties can have documentation issues.

For example, some land plots are only owned by contract and not have official land registry, or any constructions not being officially registered on the land. Make sure that your agent proves that all documentation is in perfect order or fully explains if any outstanding issues.

LAND

Land has traditionally been one of the best forms of investment and in countries such as Brazil, the wealthy have found land to be a safe investment against inflation.

The Brazilian economy is now showing strong fundamentals such as low inflation, strong growth, falling interest rates and declining unemployment/rising basic pay. All of these factors are driving up real estate prices just as in the other BRIC economies.

Many people invest profitably in land by adopting one of the following strategies.

Land Banking/Speculation - Investing in land in an area where the local area is being redeveloped or rezoned. Demand is especially strong when the economy is developing as demand increases and the supply is finite.

Small Development - Buy individual plot(s) and build a house. This is a good route for those seeking to start as a property developer to build their own home for a fraction of the value. For example if you buy a small plot and build a small house your total investment could be around €40,000 and you could resell for around €50,000 excluding capital appreciation.

Land Redevelopment - This is ideal for the large investor who buys a large piece of land and gets planning permission and develops the site. - Value creation occurs when a piece of land is developed and becomes useful to someone. Obtaining planning permission and developing your land is a sure way to add value. The increase in value is a function of the location and the development plan.

In Brazil, buying plots is much more common than the UK,USA and EUROPE. Historically the well-off have preferred to have a bespoke designed home and the less well-off have found it cheaper because of the lack of availability of finance and mortgages.

Established models, such as those from companies like Alphaville prove that the land development model in Brazil works and is very profitable. Alphaville masterplan, zone and develop the infrastructure to sell residential and commercial lots within their gated developments for around US$100 per square metre. They are perhaps one of the best known land development companies in Brazil and are currently developing almost 15,467 plots across Brazil.

Recent success stories include the Alphaville Natal where demand was so high, over 900 plots were sold in only 16 hours. After development capital growth is also strong in good quality developments. In Alphaville Fortaleza; plot owners saw price appreciation of over 80.4% in the 20 months following the launch of the project.

Compared with UK,USA and Europe prices, prime sites (beachfront or city centre) in Brazil are still relatively cheap. However not all land is equal in terms of investment potential.

Did you know that...?

Forests cover 65% of the territory? In Brazil is the biggest tropical pluvial forest of the world: the Amazon, with its rare plants also used in modern medicine?

Also, in Brazil animal species are amongst the widest raging of the world?

Brazil has the greatest biological diversity in the world?
There are:
• 55,000 plant species;
• 524 mammal species;
• 517 amphibian species;
• 1,622 bird species;
• 468 reptile species;
• 3,000 freshwater fish species

A extensão geográfica da Area Protegida sob as unidades de conservação brasileiras, que soma 755.508 km², é maior do que os estados americanos da Califórnia, de Washington e de Nova York juntos, com seus 737,078 km² ?

That in the northeast the landscape is typically tropical with extremely white beaches surrounded by magnificent palms and by the warm sea?

That according to the World Bank, Brazil, India and China will turn into the nations having the highest rate of growth in the next 25 years?

That Brazil is the eight global economy with a GDP of US$ 840 billion?

That it's the 1st global producer of coffee, oranges and sugarcane? The 2nd of manioc, beans, beef and poultry? The 3rd of sugar and corn? The 2nd global exporter of chickens and the 4th of pork?

That It's the 2nd global producer of ironstones, the 5th of manganese, the 6th of aluminum, the 7th of gold and the eight of tin?

That Brazil owns the 6th greatest iron reserve of the world?

The GDP of Argentina is equal to the GDP of the State of Sao Paulo?

The greatest hydroelectric power station of the world is Itaipu?

That Brazil occupies the tenth position in the world as electric energy producer?

That Brazil owns the tenth largest industrial park of the world?

That it's the 7th country of the world for amount of computers and the greatest global market of information technology?

That Brazil is in first place for the number of users of "Internet banking" overcoming Canada, the USA and Japan?

That it's the first global manufacturer of ceramics coatings and compressors for refrigeration, the 4th of beer, the 5th of flue, the 6th of cigarettes, the 7th of fridges?

That Brazil is the pioneer in divisions such as aeronautic engineering, high oil-bearing technology, development of satellites, enrichment of uranium and vaccines?

That Brazil is the only country of the Southern Hemisphere that takes part of the Genoma Project?

That it's the 3rd global manufacturer of aircrafts for regional flights and for training?

That the Brazilian company Embraer is the 4th global manufacturer of commercial aircraft?

That EMBRAER sells turboprop-reaction aircrafts in countries such as USA, France, Italy, Switzerland, Portugal, Spain, United Kingdom and China?

That in 1997 it just 0,7% of GDP was invested in technological development and that, nowadays, this rate has increased to 1,8%?

That Brazil is in 9th place among the countries that use the internet the most, after USA, Japan, United Kingdom, China, Canada, South Corea and Italy?

That the 65% of websites in Latin America are Brazilian?

That Brazilian television has been the 4th in the world broadcasting daily, after USA, United Kingdom and France?

That Globo TV is the 4th television station, overcome only by the three great stations of North America (ABC, CBC e NBC)?

That unemployment rates are lower than European ones (Italy:12%) and was 4,8% in December of 2000?

That editorial market of books, with 50.000 annual titles, is greater than in Italy?

That Brazil is the 12th global manufacturer of cars (Audi, Chrysler, Fiat, Ford, General Motors, Honda, Mercedes, Peugeot, Renault, Toyota, and Volkswagen)?

That in 2002, 95% of Brazilians sent their declaration of income tax via Internet?

That during the last elections 65% of votes were made with electronic systems and that 67.000 new ballot-boxes showed the candidates' pictures?

100 millions votes have been scrutinized in 24 hours?

That in the northeast 70% of properties that are more expensive than 50.000 reais are bought by Europeans?

That in the north east the airports of Natal, Recife e Fortaleza together receive 105 international flights per week arriving from Europe, two times more than they received in 2003?

That these 105 flights arrive directly from the major Europeans' capital cities, non-stop, and that it takes 6 hours flying from Lisbon?

A European in the northeast almost triplicates the purchasing power of his money due to the favorable exchange rate from Euro into real?

In the last 3 years in the northeast the amount of Europeans that have decided to buy a house or to start a new life, usually opening lodging or a restaurant, has increased by 60%?

That with the same amount of money needed to buy a 100 m2 apartment in Madrid, a Spanish retired person can buy a two floor mansion with 4 suites in front of the beach in northeast Brazil?

That an increasing number of Europeans living in flats in their country are enchanted by the opportunity of buying huge houses, at few metres from the beach, where the sun is always shining and there is always a fisherman offering tasty lobster for 17 reais.

Official and commercial language

The official language is Portuguese but, frequently, English and Spanish are also used for negotiations.

Weights and measures

Metric.

Official festivities and schedules

Anyone who thinks of events and holidays in Brazil almost simultaneously thinks of Carnival. Whilst Carnival does indeed play a major part in the events and holidays of Brazil, with a population in which approximately one in every two is Roman Catholic, and from a continent famous for *fiesta*, it should come as no surprise to learn that Brazil has a number of events and holidays in addition to the world famous Carnival.

Brazil's Events and Holidays include:

New Year's Day (December 31 - January 1)

New Year's Day is known as Ano Novo (Portuguese) locally, but is probably more famously known as Reveillon. Whilst the whole country celebrates New Year's Day, as with most major festivals in Brazil, the place to be on New Year's Day is Rio de Janeiro - where anywhere up to 2 million people gather to revel in an all night / all day party. If you want to join in the fun and frolics of Rio on New Year's Eve, take yourself off to Copacabana beach where you can join in with some of the best fireworks and live music in South America!

Carnival Rio (late February - early March)

Carnival Rio takes place during the 5 day up to Ash Wednesday, with the last day of Carnival falling on Shrove Tuesday. Although the most famous events during the 5 days of Carnival are the Rio Carnival, events celebrating Carnival take place all over the country. Visitors to Brazil should keep in mind that all 5 days of Rio Carnival are public holidays all over Brazil - therefore most shops will be closed during the period covering Carnival Rio. Traditionally, this is also the culmination of the Brazilian summer holidays and Carnival Rio also marks the end of the long school holidays (which start in December). As a result, travel during Rio Carnival time can be difficult.

Good Friday (March/April)

As a predominately Roman Catholic nation, Good Friday is a national holiday in Brazil.

Easter Sunday (March/April)

Easter Sunday, following Good Friday is a holiday in Brazil; but Easter Monday is not.

Tiradentes Day (April 21)

Tiradentes Day in Brazil commemorates the execution of Brazilian national hero Joaquim Jose da Silva Xavier - a co-conspirator in the 1789 revolt against the Portuguese. If you are wondering how this holiday gets its name, "tiradentes" means "tooth-puller", and Xavier was a dentist by trade.

Labor Day (May 1)

As with elsewhere in the world, Labor Day is celebrated in Brazil on May 1, and is one of the national holidays in Brazil.

Corpus Christi (June 10)

Another of the Brazilian holidays signifying its close association with the Roman Catholic Church.

Independence Day (September 7)

Dom Pedro officially declared Brazil's independence from Portugal on this day in 1822.

Our Lady of Aperecida Day (October 12)

Nossa Senhora de Aperecida is the patron saint of Brazil and this national holiday in Brazil is dedicated to her.

All Souls' Day (November 2)

As with other traditional Roman Catholic countries, All Souls' Day is a public holiday in Brazil.

Republic Day (November 15)

Almost ironically, Republic Day is celebrated in Brazil to commemorate the day in 1889 when Dom Pedro - hero of Independence Day - was removed from power.

Christmas (December 25)

Christmas in Brazil officially starts on December 24, which is a half-day holiday. Christmas Day itself is locally known as Feliz Natal. Those deciding to celebrate Christmas in Brazil should note that Christmas is actually the height of the summer season here - so you're unlikely to see Santa in snow gear, and far more likely to see him on a Jet Ski off the coast of Rio!

Other important events and holidays in Brazil include:

Washing of the Steps of Bonfim Church (3rd Thursday in January)

In a deeply religious country, this Brazil event constitutes one of the most significant events in the Brazilian calendar. The event itself occurs in Salvador and comprises of hundreds of women in traditional Bahian dress carrying perfumed water to wash the church's steps. Careful though, this event can attract up to 800,000 onlookers!

Founding of Rio de Janeiro Day (January 20)

As with all festivals held in Rio - another spectacular occasion.

Founding of Sao Paulo Day (January 25)

The city of Sao Paulo is Brazil's largest and over 20 million people celebrate this day!

Discovery Day (April 22)

Commemorates the day in 1500 on which Brazil is said to have been discovered by Pedro Alvarez Cabral.

Lovers' Day (June 12)

Anyone who is familiar with Valentine's Day will know this festival. Exactly the same concept - just a different date.

Shops

Shops are open from Monday to Friday from 9.00 am to 5.30/7.00 PM.
On Saturdays the shops are open until 2.00 PM, with the exception of those situated in shopping centers that shut at 10.00 PM.
On Sundays almost all the commercial activities are shut, with the exception of many shopping centers.

Banking & Currency

From Monday to Friday, from 10.00 am to 4.00 pm, or from 09.00 am to 3.00 PM during the summertime.

Brazil's currency is the real. According to US securities firm, Merrill Lynch, the real is the best-placed currency in Latin America to weather increased risk aversion caused by the ongoing turmoil in global financial markets.

According to the IMF, the real's record strength against the US dollar during 2007 allowed Brazil to accumulate reserves. Its US$200 billion in foreign exchange reserves and the central bank's market interventions is likely to keep the Brazilian currency steady for most of 2009.

The Central Bank of Brazil closely monitors the economy and financial situation, and in April 2009, it cut its benchmark interest rate (Selic rate) to 10.25%.

According to the IMF, Brazil's financial sector is generally sound and it has praised the measures being taken to limit risk-taking practices.

Bring along currency

American dollar and Euro are the most used currencies, both in hotels and in banks. The limit for outgoing currency is about 9.620 Euro. However it is recommended to declare amounts over <u>10.000 Reais or the equivalent in other currency.</u>

Climate

Seasons are opposite of European ones with the exception of Northern and Northeastern ones where climate is tropical.

In Rio de Janeiro and in the northern/north east states we suggest summer and spring clothes for the Brazilian wintertime that goes from July to September. In Rio the average temperature reaches the minimum level of 15°/20°C.

In the summertime the average temperature is higher than 35°C.

We suggest summer and winter or half season clothes for the period between July and September for the State of Sao Paolo, Middle-North/Middle west and Southern States, where the thermal excursion during the day can decrease from 18 to 0°C.

During the summertime (November/march) also in these states the average temperature is about 30°C.

Unlike many exotic sunshine destinations around the world, Brazil is a country that you can visit any time of the year and has never been particularly expensive. Indeed, with the Internet offering discount flights to Brazil the only limiting factors you may have when deciding when to go to Brazil are the reasons you wish to visit Brazil (its mega-metropolis, delightful beaches, or amazing Amazon rainforest) and deciding whether or not you wish to travel the country extensively. To help you decide when to go to Brazil we set out some of the main events in a Brazilian year.

In the event that you would like to travel around Brazil, it is generally suggested that visitors do not travel during the months of December to February as this is when the Brazilian school system is on its long summer vacation. As a result, a large number of Brazilians are themselves traveling domestically during this time - resulting in accommodation and domestic travel being both at a premium and difficult to arrange. Beside this limitation, it is also generally accepted that travel to the south of Brazil should not be undertaken during the same period as temperatures can reach forty degrees Celsius and the humidity during this time makes the south unbearably sticky for many. The south should also be avoided during the rainy season (June to August) as it tends to be a period of continuous rain!

Those wishing to visit Brazil for carnival will need to make arrangements to visit Brazil in late February early March - depending on when Easter is that year, as carnival takes place during the 5 days up to Ash Wednesday (the last day of carnival is actually on Shrove Tuesday).

Travel in and around Brazil can also be difficult during the following annual events:

* New Year: December 31 - January 1 - known locally as Ano Novo. Accommodation in Rio de Janeiro can be especially difficult to find during this period as up to 2 million people gather to party the night away.
* Carnival Rio: late February - early March - when finding accommodation anywhere in Brazil can be difficult.
* Independence Day: September 7 - fortunately, unlike carnival, this is only a one-day event as the whole country comes to a standstill!

If you are visiting Brazil with the intention of visiting some of Brazil's pristine beaches, keep in mind that Brazil's beaches are on the Atlantic coast and so you should try to avoid traveling during the months of June to August, when the sea can be notoriously rough and cold. Also bear in mind that a number of tourists to Brazil's beaches each year drown in the coastal waters of Brazil as they haven't taken into consideration the local reefs, currents and under-tones.

Transportation

The public transportation network can't vouch for good maintenance, with the exception of the subway, which is only present in the big cities (Sao Paulo and Rio), where the quality of the service reaches the highest standards in the world.

Taxis, are available in great quantities and usually with a modern and adequate fleet of vehicles, at any time of the day and of the night.

With the vast size of Brazil, however, the biggest question is how should one travel around Brazil if one wants to travel Brazil safely. If this is you concern, the following are the generally accepted modes of transport in Brazil:

Brazil Transportation - Air travel

Approximately the same size as continental United States, flights to Brazil are well served from North America, Europe and Asia. Here, ordinarily flights to Brazil that originate in North America, Europe or Asia frequently fly to Rio de Janeiro (the city famous for its carnival), Sao Paulo (the country's most populace city) and Brasilia (the capital). Cheap flights to Brazil, through all of these gateways, are also freely available.

Aside from these, both full-fare and cheap flights to Brazil arrive at two of Brazil's favorite other holiday destinations, Recife (a popular package tourist destination) and Manaus (located right in the heart of the Amazon basin).

Once in Brazil, travel in Brazil is fairly accessible, but is not cheap - when considered against the cheap flights available into Brazil. Having said this, provided that you are willing to shop around a number of travel agents, you should be able to locate some cheap flights in Brazil; and if you want to see anything of the country, you'll need to take at least one domestic flight in Brazil - as the country is so large! For those looking to do extensive travel in Brazil, a Brazil Airpass, from Varig or Tam, can be purchased with international flights to Brazil. However, do keep in mind that both Varig and Tam Airpasses can be purchased once you have arrived in Brazil, and once you have decided how much travel in Brazil you want to do. Normally though you can save yourself a substantial amount of money if you purchase your Varig or Tam Airpass as part of your overall ticket price for your international flight to Brazil.

Brazil's national airline is Varig, which flies both domestically and internationally. Many of the cheap flights to Brazil, and flights within Brazil, can be purchased with Varig. Varig is an especially good option to fly to Brazil with if you intend to do any domestic travel in Brazil.

One note of caution should be kept in mind when purchasing cheap flights to Brazil, both international flights that travel out of Brazil, and domestic flights that travel in Brazil, are subject to departure tax. Normally these taxes are included in the ticket price. However, the international and domestic departure taxes are not cheap, so some travel agents adopt a policy of not including these sums in their flight prices in an attempt to make their cheap flights to Brazil look more attractive.

A final word of caution is that Brazil immigration rules require all passengers arriving on flights to Brazil to have passports with expiry dates exceeding 6-months. Consequently, if you arrive on a flight to Brazil with a passport that has less than 6-months till it expires, you may well find yourself facing a real problem. Also, nearly all non-Brazilian nationals and citizens are required to obtain a visa in order to travel to Brazil. Generally these travel Brazil visas are for 90-days, extendable for a further 90-days.

Brazil transportation – Bus

As is the case in other South American countries, Brazilian's love to travel on buses, which are a primary means of cheap transportation around the country. Consequently, buses in Brazil usually comes with an excellent and reliable service. Also, unlike other modes of transportation, buses in Brazil can transport you from all the major cities and towns, including right into the heart of the Amazon jungle. In this regard, bus journey in some of the more remote areas of

Brazil have been known to have accidents, especially at night - so do be careful. Here, as a general comment, whilst Brazil's bus service is excellent, Brazil's roads (safety-wise) leave a lot to be desired.

Tourists traveling on any of the buses within any of the major cities should prepare themselves for long traffic jams! And, if you travel anywhere by road in San Paulo, expect to take some time over the journey as the roads here crawl 24 hours a day, 7 days a week!

Brazil transportation - Train

Train enthusiasts should already know before they arrive which Brazilian train line to select from, since most trains in Brazil these days are under serviced and lack real investment. Having said this, South America, and Brazil in particular, offer some of the most picturesque train journeys available anywhere in the world, so you may want to try the trains in Brazil after all - especially the Curitiba-Paranagua line, which is delightful!

Brazil transportation - Car hire

It is generally accepted that tourists should not hire cars in Brazil unless they know what they're doing! Road safety in Brazil is not the best in the world, and the standard of driving here leaves a lot to be desired. However, there are a number of car hire agencies operating in Brazil, so if you want to rent a car here it is feasible. But, do travel/drive with a good map and plenty of water.

Finding the right Brazil Rental Car when you're traveling can be quite a challenge but there are many companies that can provide pricing online and allow booking over the internet. Experiences with rental cars in vary from city to city, but getting a grasp on the basic steps will help make it easier getting car rentals while you're out visiting the various regions in Brazil.

Europe and the US are places where the process of getting rental cars is a smooth and overall uniform experience. However, in other countries an auto rental experience can be challenging and chaotic. No matter where you are visiting from, the following tips will prove useful if you're planning to hire one of the rental cars in Brazil.

1. Aside from knowing how long your trip is going to be, you might want to at least have a rough plan for where you take the car rental. Calculate the driving and sightseeing time so that you have the car for as long as you would actually need it. Once you've determined

this, you are ready to start planning where and how you are going to find the best rental cars in Brazil.

2. Obtain or make sure your current drivers license will be valid during the period you will be driving any car rentals. You may want to obtain an international drivers license as well if you plan on booking car rentals, it is valid in all the member countries of the United Nations. If you unsure whether or not the country you are visiting is a United Nations be sure you do a little research before your trip.

3.Contact a travel agent at least a month prior to the date you need the car rental. You need to tell them where you are planning to take the rent car, along with the dates you would like to have the auto rental. It's also easy and simple to look on the Internet, where you can easily compare rates or book reservations.

4. Mainly you get to select the vehicle class, size and dates for your automobile rental. Also, this is where you determine what locations you are planning to drop off the auto rental. If this location is different than where you are picking it up, there is going to be a fee, depending on the country.

5. Pay for your deposit if it is required.

6. Brush up on traffic signs and driving laws for the country you plan on visiting.

The ease with which you can rent a car in a country can vary based on regulations, rates availability and driving conditions. You generally do not have the flexibility to travel in between countries in rental cars, especially in South America. Generally, however, if you have a valid license, a passport, a major credit card, and you are over 25, you are able to book rental cars in Brazil. Another factor to consider is the driving hazards. In undeveloped and third world countries traffic laws are not followed or enforced regularly. Drivers are very aggressive. To some degree you will have to adjust your driving style, but not to such an extent that you end up in a traffic accident. That will be a major headache to deal with in a car rental from another country.

These are the main steps to keep in mind. These other smaller aspects of an automobile rental; but are also important factors to consider.

Insurance for rental cars:

If you pay for the car rental with a credit card, it may also cover insurance, but it will only be valid for 30 days. If you have auto insurance of your own, it will not be valid for the car you are renting.

Returning rental cars in Brazil:

You car is going to be inspected carefully when you return it, so make sure you look over your car rentals yourself before you leave and report any signs of damage to the company.

Some of the larger brand name rental car companies are listed below but most often cheap car rentals can be found by using the smaller companies.

Alamo

Avis

Budget

Dollar

Enterprise

Hertz

National Car

Brazil transportation- Boat/river travel

Those who enjoy a little more adventurous form of transportation might want to consider taking one of the boat ferries through some of the most spectacular, dense, vegetation in Brazil aboard a boat/ferry. Boats and ferries in Brazil traditionally trade their wares along the inland waterways of Brazil, and if you have time this is a recommended mode of Brazilian transportation.

GEOGRAFIC POSITION

Brazil is situated in South America, It's surrounded by Venezuela, Guyana, Surename, French Guyana, Uruguay, Argentina, Paraguay, Peru, Bolivia and Colombia.

AREA

8.511.965 km2 (the fifth biggest Country of the world)

POPULATION

About 187.552.000 source www.ibge.gov.br - IBGE - Istituto Brasileiro di Geografia e Statística.

LANGUAGE

Portuguese is the official language of Brazil but the one spoken in Brazil has a different accent and intonation from the Portuguese spoken in Portugal. Also there are other languages spoken by Indian tribes living in reserves.

DOCUMENTS

An entry visa isn't required to enter Brazil. A passport, with a minimum remaining validity of 6 months from the leaving date, needs to be shown to the customs' police plus a return ticket. The tourist visa, valid for 90 days will be issued at arrival, Keep copy of the application form because it will need to be returned when leaving.

CREDIT CARDS

The main international credit cards are accepted in hotels, in shops and restaurants.

TIME ZONE

-4 hours from Italy. During the summer time the difference is of 3 – 5 hours.

Temperatures

Temperatures hover around 28°C year-round in the North and Northeast region and are around 20ºC in the South.There are places in the South of Brazil where in winter temperatures reach 0°C.

PHONE CALLS

From Brazil to United Kingdom: 0021 + 44 + local code + phone number

Mobiles 0021 + 44 + nº telefônico

From United kingdom to Brazil: 0055 + local code + phone number

Mobiles 0055 + local code + phone number

SHOPPING

Beyond the famous precious stones, the offer of the awesome summer sensual and colored fashion is what reflects most the spirit of Brazil, especially the beach fashion with its great choice of t-shirts and tanga bikinis known all over the world. Handcrafts are one more option suggested for presents or personal shopping. Objects made of straw, ceramics, terracotta, nuts and wood and represent the uniqueness and the tradition of every region.

Wonderful lace tablecloths can be found in the North east of Brazil. You can't miss buying Brazilian music CDs.

SPORT

The passion that Brazilians have for sport is shown by the existance of about 8.000 athletic teams all over Brazil and the most widespread sport is certainly soccer, called "futebol".

POPULATION

In Brazil people are friendly and cordial. You will discover the magic of Brazil trough the free and nationalistic spirit of Brazilians, which is a mix of romanticism and beauty known all over the world.

SHORT HISTORY

Brazil was discovered on the 22nd of April 1500 by a Portuguese sailor Pedro Alvares Cabral. The name BRAZIL comes from a type of wood called "pau brazil" from which a red tint for clothes' coloration used to be extracted.

In 1822 the Prince of Portugal proclaimed Brazil officially an independent country.

In 1889 after a monarchic-economical crisis, a Republic was proclaimed. Nowadays the President is the head of the state, he's designated and elected by the population and he's in charge for five years.

CUISINE

Portuguese cuisine brought by colonizers has been developed in a tropical environment, it has joined the new natives' traditions and eventually has received the influence of the ingredients used by African slaves, that's how Brazilian cuisine was created. "Feijoada" is considered the typical Brazilian dish. It was created in Rio de Janeiro.

Meat in Brazil is excellent and in "churrascarias" it's served broiled in big and tasty portions, as it used to be in the whole country. Along the coast there are different ways to prepare seafood, with many recipes of fish, shrimps and the wonderful lobster of the Northeast.

The huge quantity of fruit, served naturally or in juices and colored shakes, is available everywhere. Every region of Brazil is a real festival of tastes, aromas and tasty delights. Eating in Brazil is very convenient there are a great choice of restaurants of different categories where you can eat very well.

As a cosmopolitan country, the majority of Brazil's main cities offer tourists a wide variety of international cuisines. As it happens, eating out in Brazil is also a very affordable experience, with superb service. However, most visitors to a country want to delve into the local dishes at least once during their stay, and the following are some the national Brazilian foods you'll see in nearly any restaurants in Brazil:

* Feijoada - the national dish of Brazil, this Brazilian food will be served to you whether you chose to eat in one of the many Brazil restaurants, or if you are more adventurous and chose to eat on the street. Feijoada is a delicious combination of rice, black beans and pork. Having said that you can get this traditional Brazilian food in any restaurant, the best time to eat this in any restaurants in Brazil is on a Sunday, as this the traditional time to eat this.

* Caipirinha - caipirinha is the national drink that is normally drank by diners in most Brazil restaurants prior to eating their Feijoada.

Caipirinha is a potent, delicious lime and sugar can drink - very refreshing for the tropics!

* Caldo - Caldo is a soup dish that restaurants in Brazil normally serve before the main dish - Feijoada.

Beside these national dishes and drink, restaurants in Brazil cater for the serious meat eater, known locally Churrascarias - an all you can eat meat restaurant! However, Brazil is probably as famous for its coffee as it is for Carnival and no trip to Brazil would be complete without at least one sample of the local brew. Visitors need to be aware though that Brazilians take their coffee very strong, sweet and in small cups. Also, Brazilian culture dictates that if someone offers you a cup of coffee, you cannot refuse such an offer.

As a tropical country with dense forestation, it should be no surprise that Brazilian food also comprises of a vast array of wonderful, tasty, splendid fruits of types and sizes. So, whilst in a Brazilian restaurant, try out the cupuacu, bacuri, caju, umbu and açai.

Brazilians are fairly favorable to the idea of going to a Brazil restaurants specializing in sweets (desserts). Here, ordinary Brazilians take themselves off to a lanchonetes (snack bar) or paradise (bakery) to savor some of the finer elements of Brazilian food.

If you are traveling in or around the Manaus area, make sure you take full advantage of eating some of the local Brazilian food, as the

Brazilian food in this region has been heavily influenced by African cuisine.

Finally, Brazilians end to enjoy drinking "chooppe" when socializing. Choppe is a locally brewed beer, which has a heavy Germanic influence in its taste. Beside this, Brazilians out enjoying themselves like to drink Caipirinha.

So, no matter where you dine out in Brazil, and regardless of whether or not you want to eat Brazilian food, restaurants in Brazil are both inexpensive and the center of some great socializing - so enjoy a night out in one of the many Brazil restaurants!

MUSIC

Brazil is considered a musical country! It has always been characterized by a big diversity and thanks to musical influences coming from three continents, it's always developing new and original styles. Samba is still influencing other rhythms such as the recent "pagode", which is slower and more passionate. Carmen Miranda is probably the most famous export; she was popular for her hot temperament and for her fruit-blow off. Bossa nova, quieter and influenced by the northern American jazz, became popular in the fifties thanks to musicians such as João Gilberto and songs such as "The girl of Ipanema". Tropicalism appeared in Brazil more or less during the sixties and its founders were artists such as

Caetano Veloso and Gilberto Gil. Its offers a mix of different musical styles including typical Italian songs that used to talk about the Brazilian government of that period. More recently axè music, created by bands of Bahia, has become very popular.

CAPOEIRA

A mix of dance and fighting, Capoeira was created in Brazil by the slaves, according to African traditions, to defend themselves from physical aggressions and threats. During the years this dance/fight has been enriched with new movements and variations. It uses malice and the creativity of the arms, legs, hands, feet, elbows shoulders and knees as weapons. In Capoeira not only fighters but also musicians have an important role, especially the one that plays berimbau who directs the fight with his rhythm.

CARNIVAL

The most relevant expression of the art and the traditional culture and the most well-known party of Brazil is the Carnival, that lasts one month with dances and crazynesses and that is celebrated in the whole country. The most famous is certainly the carnival of Rio de Janeiro with its parades inside the Sambodromo, a street boarded by stands deliberately installed, where the best school of sambas of the city make a parade, every year they offer a unique show. In November in Natal a very famous out of season carnival called "CARNATAL" takes place.

CANDOMBLE'

A Religion brought by African slaves that offers adoration to the "orixás", considered spirits of the nature that come from fire, from the earth, from water and from the air, they can be kings or queens of Africa or other special characters that were in the power of protection.

In the beginning its rituals were practiced in the "senzalas", where the slaves used to live, or in the fields around the "fazendas" where they used to work. Nowadays they are revered in secret ceremonies and the parties all year long, always accompanied by the "filhos-de-santo" that, wearing typical outfits, enter into a trance and incorporate the spirits of "orixas". There are divisions of Candomblé in different locations of Brazil and it is curious that it is practiced by a great number of Catholics. However, a match exists between every "orixás" of Candomblé with the saints of the catholic religion.

FEDERATIVE REPUBLIC OF BRAZIL

executive branch

Head of state and Government: Luiz inácio Lula da Silva

Vice-President: josé Alencar

Ministers chosen by the president

Election: the President and vice president are elected by popular vote to a mandate of four years, and can seek reelection.

legislative Branch

congress is made up of the Senate (81 senators elected by a majority vote to a mandate of 8 years) and the chamber of deputies (513 deputies elected by proportional vote to a mandate of 4 years).

Judicial Branch

judicial Branch agencies: Supreme court (constitutional court);

Superior court of justice;

Federal regional courts and Federal judges;

Labor courts and judges; Electoral courts and judges;

Military courts and judges and Federal, State and territorial courts and judges.

capital

Brasília, located in the Federal district (GMt - 3 hours)

Brazil in key figures

Life expectancy

Total population: 73.49 years

Men: 69.5 years

Women: 77.95 years

(2007 – estimate)

Ethnic Groups

Whites: 49.9%

Mixed-race: 43.2%

Blacks: 6.3%

Asian: 0.7%

(2005 – PNAD)

Religions

Catholic: 73.6%

Protestant: 15.4%

Others: 1.6%

International environmental agreements

Antarctic-Environmental Protocol,

Antarctic-Marine Living Resources,

Antarctic Seals, Antarctic Treaty,

Biodiversity, Climate Change, Climate

Change-Kyoto Protocol, etc.

National flag

Brazil's national flag was created, in 1889, by Raimundo Teixeira Mendes and Miguel Lemos, based on a design by Décio Vilares. Inspired by the Imperial flag, designed by the French painter Jean-Baptiste Debret, it has a celestial blue sphere and the positivist motto "Order and Progress" in place of the imperial crown.

Inflation (consumer price index – IPCA)

2008 5.90%

2007 4.50%

2006 3.14%

2005 5.69%

2004 7.60%

2003 9.30%

2002 12.53%

2001 7.67%

2000 5.97%

Ethanol

Most sugarcane is cultivated in the southeast region of Brazil, 2,500 km from the Amazon, the equivalent of a trip from Rome to Moscow. In all, 90% of sugarcane production for ethanol is found in the Southeast, Central and South of Brazil.

The United Nations' Food and Agriculture Organization, the FAO, singles out Brazilian ethanol as the least expensive of any country, and Brazil as the only country capable of producing this fuel competitively and without subsidies.

Daily petroleum production

- 2.4 million barrels/day
- World leader in deepwater petroleum exploration
- One of the 10 largest reserves in the world (Tupi Field)

Electricity generation

- Capacity: 102,000 megawatts (MW) in 2008
- Leader in renewable and clean energy: 44% of energy derived from renewable sources.　The world average is 14%
- World's largest exporter of ethanol and third largest for biodiesel

Computers

50 million

Internet users

- 40 million
- Largest number of Internet users in Latin America and 11th in the world

Time spent on the Internet

- World leader, with 23h48m per month
- 50% of the social networking sites on Orkut are Brazilian
- World's largest user of instant messaging on MSN

Cell phones

Sixth largest market in the world, with 150 million subscribers

Notes:

CONTACT:

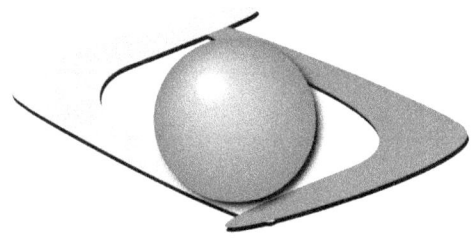

www.brazilrealproperty.com

info@brazilrealproperty.com

brazilrealproperty

msn: msn@brazilrealproperty.com